M000312355

A CALL TO MASTERY

Living the Art of Ascension

Paula K. Bronte

First printing 2008
EAN 978-0-9791317-2-1, ISBN 0-9791317-2-3

Contact Paula Bronte at:
www.acalltomastery.com
acalltomastery@yahoo.com

Photo of the author by Faren Bachelis.

Attention Corporations, Universities, Colleges, and Professional Organizations: Quantity discounts are available on bulk purchases of this book for educational, gift purposes, or as premiums. Special books or book excerpts can also be created to fit specific needs. For information, please contact RealityIs Books, an imprint of RealityIsBooks.com, Inc., 309 E. Rand Road, Unit 313, Arlington Heights, IL 60004. Tel: 866-534-3366, Email: publish@RealityIsBooks.com.

ACKNOWLEDGMENTS

My heartfelt and eternal gratitude goes to:

All that is divine—my beloved "I Am" presence and the great beings of light who assisted in writing this work, especially Beloved Cassiopeia and Mighty Mercury.

My spiritual teachers, especially Shri Mataji Nirmala Devi.

The numerous authors of spiritual and metaphysical works who have offered themselves as channels for divine wisdom—their teachings have helped shape my life.

My Rapid Eye Technology teachers, especially Dr. Ranae Johnson.

My Peace Corps friends who, with love and patience, assisted in proofing this work: Shuva Rahim, Valeri Bowman, John Bowman, Peter Woods, and Crystal Woods.

My remarkable and devoted friends Ann Darling and Barbara Borchers whose loving letters and consistent correspondence saw me through the two years of my Peace Corps service.

Diane Cocker, she has my deep appreciation for her constant and humorous presence of love, wisdom, and power.

Faren Bachelis for her contributions to this book including photography, editing and content commentary. Her artistic skills are matched only by her loving heart and powerful spirit.

My dear, sweet brother Joe Bronte, for always being my dear, sweet brother.

To my divine partner, Anold Lane, for the intimacy, joy, and loving appreciation that feeds my soul and fills my world.

I love you all.

And special thanks to Jim Loftus at RealityIsBooks.com for his patient support, expertise, and professionalism in editing and publishing this work.

CONTENTS

INTRODUCTION

I expected silence here, in the South American jungle.

I expected clean, unpolluted air. I expected fresh, exotic fruits and plenty of vegetables. But when I rise in the morning, I hear huge trucks rolling along the unpaved Afabakka Highway.

In my backyard, as I lounge in my hammock, I hear the penetrating songs and sounds of birds—countless birds, unknowable in the shelter of the jungle trees.

I breathe, not fresh, rain-forest oxygen, but red dirt and auto exhaust of the highway.

I eat canned vegetables and peanut butter.

I expected to love this place and my time here. I am shocked at the depth of my love, my appreciation—my full acceptance of this place and my time here.

I remember reading once that as soon as we fall in love with someone we begin to worry about losing them, thus tainting (or defining) the sheer ecstasy of in-love-ness. My mind tries to secretly tiptoe toward the thoughts of "Only two years—it will be over too fast," and "What if I waste the time?" I can, sometimes successfully, throw a lasso around those renegade thoughts and reel them back through the turnstile of recreation. I wring them out and hang them in the face of shining gratitude for what is here and what is now.

I suppose there are some people who couldn't live in this environment. There are not a lot of activities to reflect how important you are or how needed you are or that will protect you from your own painful memories.

We have pineapple plants here. Did you know pineapples are the most inexplicable shade of pink when they're babies? Do you suppose they're all girls?

A hummingbird just fluttered around a pink baby, then fluttered away.

The hummingbird, pineapple, and countless creatures of this place all know why they are here. They have their purpose and they live in the rhythm of their usefulness.

Perhaps some people would envy them for their certainty. As for me, my certainty wavers less each day. I am here to serve in Suriname as a Peace Corps volunteer. Beyond that, I am here to free my attention for the uninterrupted worship of all that is divine and to write this book, if that divinity will write it through me.

I am here, on the road to mastery and ascension.

Now, if only I could just get these damn bugs to stop biting ...

* * *

I have waited many years to write this book. I have doubted, second-guessed, and talked myself out of it. I tell myself it's too much, a mountain too high to climb. I tell myself all I have to offer has already been offered by so many others—others who are much wiser and more enlightened than me. What I teach and use in my practice and lectures comes from numerous sources. A plethora of psychological and spiritual writings, teachings, and philosophies weaves through my way of being in the world.

Twenty years ago a wonderful teacher, a woman who gave lessons called "A Course in Miracles," once shared with me that she wanted to write a book. "But, there are already so many books," she said. I immediately retorted with convincing arguments about the fact that she has her own insights and gifts to share. We can read several different books, all conveying the same message, but one or two will resonate and the rest not so much. One or two may speak directly to us in a way that seeps into our cells and transforms our hearts and minds. How many times, since that day twenty years ago, have I replayed that conversation, unable or unwilling to heed my own advice?

The radiation of an individual pours out through not only the physical presence, but all a person says, does, and creates (including the writing of books). It's all about vibration.

So now, I come to you naked in my determination. I intend for you what I intend for myself, to be clothed only in light, to be filled only with light, to be only light.

Much of what fills the following pages are not my own thoughts, ideas, or words. Much of it may be familiar to you. Some of it may be new. But all of it reflects the vibration I have, thus far, come to be.

If that vibration should color your life with golden rays of divine love, or deepen your soul's devotion to itself, or create a momentum upon which we ride toward our ascension, then we will know in fact, we have done nothing. I will not have scripted this work, nor will you have studied it. It will have been scripted and it will have been studied by the rays of light we have always been and will forever be.

This is a book about spiritual mastery. It's written by one who is far from attaining such a state of glory, but whose only passion is to do so in this lifetime. This book is a humble, sincere, heartfelt invitation to answer the call to mastery for all who truly share in this same passion.

Through the benevolence and assistance of the ascended masters, I am consciously radiating this work with a magnetic force to attract those who are ready to step into their mastery and rise into their ascension. If you are holding this book, know you have been found out. What may be your deepest and most secret longing, though it may yet be secret even to you, is known and honored by the beings of light who direct your world. This is a call to mastery. This is a call to follow the road that will bring you to your ascension. Those, like you, who once faced the road to mastery, are now beckoning you. They chose to take that journey, and having reached their perfection, they now extend to you a loving, helping hand.

This is a journey of Devotion.

There are so many in our world today who sense, feel, believe, and desire that this lifetime be their farewell to this physical realm as we know it to be. They are seeking the way out, the way to higher ground.

This is a journey of Devotion.

Wishing, wanting, waiting is not enough to get us there. We must stand tall and walk the walk that leads us there. This is a journey of joy and love and delight, yes, but above all

This is a journey of Devotion.

Our mastery can only come to us if we choose it in full autonomy—without external cause, without dependence, without any ego-driven motive and without a backup plan if the terrain gets too rough. Our mastery is our divine right and our privilege. We have turned our backs on it for centuries, living in denial of it. In the last few decades we have turned around. Now, divine right and privilege is illumined for our recognition and available to us as it has not been for a very, very long time.

This invitation to join me on the road to mastery does have a somewhat selfish purpose. The more of us who consciously and deliberately choose to move into mastery, the better it is for all of us—and these days we need all the help we can get.

Like the story of the hundredth monkey, together we can create a critical mass upon which we may ride to our divine destination, making the journey faster and easier for us all. The power in numbers shows up here as grace. Grace can be our ticket to glory, if enough of us have the "chutzpah" to lead the way. I am betting we do. I am betting this road will take us to the biggest and best party this planet has ever seen.

Paula K. Bronte
Autumn 2004

The Hundredth Monkey
By Ken Keyes, Jr.

"The Japanese monkey, *Macaca fuscata,* had been observed in the wild for a period of over 30 years. In 1952, on the island of Koshima, scientists were providing monkeys with sweet potatoes dropped in the sand. The monkeys liked the taste of the raw sweet potatoes, but they found the dirt unpleasant. An 18-month-old female named Imo found she could solve the problem by washing the potatoes in a nearby stream. She taught this trick to her mother. Her playmates also learned this new way and they taught their mothers too. This cultural innovation was gradually picked up by various monkeys before the eyes of the scientists. Between 1952 and 1958 all the young monkeys learned to wash the sandy sweet potatoes to make them more palatable. Only the adults who imitated their children learned this social improvement. Other adults kept eating the dirty sweet potatoes. Then something startling took place. In the autumn of 1958, a certain number of Koshima monkeys were washing sweet potatoes—the exact number is not known. Let us suppose that when the sun rose one morning there were 99 monkeys on Koshima Island who had learned to wash their sweet potatoes. Let's further suppose that later that morning, the hundredth monkey learned to wash potatoes. THEN IT HAPPENED! By that evening almost everyone in the tribe was washing sweet potatoes before eating them. The added energy of this hundredth monkey somehow created an ideological breakthrough! But notice. A most surprising thing observed by these scientists was that the habit of washing sweet potatoes then jumped over the sea—Colonies of monkeys on other islands and the mainland troop of monkeys at Takasakiyama began washing their sweet potatoes. Thus, when a certain critical number achieves an awareness, this new awareness may be communicated from mind to mind. Although the exact number may vary, this Hundredth Monkey Phenomenon means that when only a limited number of people know of a new way, it may remain the conscious property of these people. But there is a point at which if only one more person tunes-in to a new awareness, a field is strengthened so that this awareness is picked up by almost everyone!"

GLOSSARY

The following is a brief explanation of this book's most frequently used terms, references, and concepts:

Ascension:

Traditionally we find this term being used in Christian religions to describe the rising of Christ up into the heavens. Most recently we are seeing an increase in the use of the word ascension among metaphysical and spiritual teachings to describe the transformation of all human consciousness into divine consciousness.

In a *New Dispensation,* Kryon describes ascension in this way: "Here's the definition of ascension: a new spiritual overlay that's so profoundly different from the energy you were born into this planet with, that it feels like, and often is, another life. Ascension is moving into the next life without dying."[1]

Ascended Master:

In her book *Archangels and Ascended Masters,* Doreen Virtue offers this definition: "A great spiritual teacher or healer who walked upon the Earth as a human, and who continues to help ... from his or her heavenly home."

The Divine:

I rely on this term to embrace all that is divine—God and Goddess, the angels, all divine beings of the heavens, the powers of nature, the points of divine light present in all matter, both animate and inanimate, and, of course, the divinity inherent within each human being.

The Higher Presence, Presence, Inner Being:

I use these terms often because our presence is as much

a part of our existence as our arm or foot—you can remove body parts, but our presence is permanent. It is almost as if a part of our actual physical self extends above us, except that part is not physical as we know physical to be and it is not a part of us; it is our wholeness. It is each person's inner being that constantly pours forth eternal love and light into and around us, thus giving us life. The presence or inner being is the individualization of the presence of God and Goddess; the actual divine power streaming right through the top of our heads working into every cell and atom of our being. It is God and Goddess manifested within each individual. This presence acts as the magnetic power that literally draws us up into the higher octaves. Presence is the engineering force inherent in our evolution toward mastery.

In such popular spiritual works as *A Course in Miracles,* this presence is referred to as the Holy Spirit. Marianne Williamson, a teacher of the principles in *A Course in Miracles,* has this to say regarding the subject:

"The Holy Spirit is not a metaphor or symbol; it is a living, alchemical power that infuses our hearts with the glory of God."[2]

Jesus:

Familiarity makes Jesus a good point of reference. Although there are thousands of other ascended beings as well, Jesus left a public legacy of words and actions. I draw upon this legacy for the purpose of illustration and clarification throughout this book.

Love:

Love, as I describe it in this book, is not about our usual experience of love. I love chocolate, I love my dog, I love it when that happens . . . These are expressions of pleasure, attachment, or the human emotion we call love. Love is the power of divinity that pours through us as unseen waves of light to heal, assist, comfort, and direct us in the art of ascension. Love is the presence of God and Goddess within us—it is who we are—whether we know it or not.

Spirituality:

Spirituality and religion are by no means mutually exclusive, but when considered separately, we see some inherent differences. A couple of these differences, in particular, are pertinent when traveling on the road to mastery.

First, we are typically driven to mainstream religions by fear, specifically the fear of death and dying. Thus, religion becomes a place of safety. Spirituality, on the other hand, is a domain of awareness. It is a place within us that seeks a relationship with ourselves as aspects of the divine. Spirituality is a consciousness driven by the loving desire to know and be who we truly are, regardless of the notion of death or what might wait for us beyond death. The conscious path of spirituality is not focused mainly on death but on life, not on fear but on love.

Second, many religions are awaiting the return of the Messiah, the Second Coming of Christ. They expect the Savior to appear again as an individual being. This concept is far too narrow. It gives the responsibility of our salvation, and therefore our spirituality, to someone other than ourselves. In so doing, it denies the magnitude of our power and our mastery. The Second Coming is the dawning of the Christ consciousness. It is a mass consciousness of divine love, wisdom, and power. It is the long anticipated fulfillment of Christ's mission. As we evolve into this consciousness, we ourselves fulfill the prophecy—*we* become the Second Coming of Christ. We need not wait for another Jesus; we need only grow into our own spiritual mastery.

"Like all the great masters, Jesus taught one thing only:

presence. Ultimate reality, the luminous, compassionate intelligence of the universe is not somewhere else, in some heaven light-years away. It didn't manifest itself any more fully to Abraham or Moses than to us, nor will it be any more present to some Messiah at the far end of time. It is what the Bible means when it says that God's true name is 'I Am.'"[3]

Vibration and the Law of Attraction:

Vibration is the speed, pattern, and movement of energy. The law of attraction states it is in the nature of vibration to seek out like vibration." That which is like unto itself is drawn."[4] The law of attraction and the concept of vibration, like many truths, have become a bit clichéd. When the truth becomes clichéd, we forget how true it is. We begin to skim the surface of some deep insights when they become too familiar. We hear them so often we tend to knead them into the fiber of our justifications; we allow ourselves to float somewhere between "what is" and "what is easier." I recently heard a line from a song—"and your lies become your truths." Be comfortable with this law and allow it to become so familiar that your life flows in harmony with it, but always acknowledge and honor its power. Know that Love is the source behind the successful implementation of the law of attraction—not greed, fear, or desperation, but love.

PART I
THE MAP

Before all else, everything begins with strengthening the spirit.

— Clarissa Pinkola Estés
Women Who Run with the Wolves

Chapter 1:
SPIRITUAL MASTERY

To become more conscious is the greatest gift anyone can give to the world; moreover, in a ripple effect, the gift comes back to its source.

— David R. Hawkins, MD
Power vs. Force

Amid our plentiful supply of writings and teachings concerning consciousness, I have noticed we seldom use the words "master" or "mastery" these days.

Maybe mastery has come to have a threatening connotation. Perhaps all its implications cause us to cower a bit. We read and hear words like "enlightened," "powerful," "evolved," or even "Christ-like" or "God-self." These expressions make us feel good. They vibrate at a high frequency; they may even stroke our egos a bit. However, these terms may shield us from the inevitability of our mastery because hidden within their ease and eloquence is the fear of that final attainment.

Wherever there is fear, we know the ego is flexing its muscles. The ego, in its precipitous effort for self-preservation, tells us it's too dangerous to go so far. Fear gives birth to selfishness; selfishness produces destruction. The last big message we received about our divine power as masters terrified us to such an extreme we crucified the messenger!

Becoming a master at anything requires deep commitment, dedicated effort, determination, and time. When we hear master musicians, we assume they have been playing for most of their lives, probably since they were quite young and for many hours a day. Their art is their life, their life is their art. That is how they achieve and maintain mastery.

Most of us don't want to work that hard at anything— even our enlightenment. We tell ourselves we will become fanatics and lose balance if we go to such an extreme. Or worse yet, we may lose our families, lovers, jobs, friends, our delicious vices and, who knows, maybe even ourselves.

Another popular mouse hole our avoidance adroitly uses for escape is the (false) humility that tells us we could never dare to compare ourselves to Christ or the other great ones. "They were masters. How can I possibly be so arrogant or blasphemous to think of myself in that way?" Well, if it is Jesus to whom we are comparing ourselves, then just a moment of analytical objectivity will close the door on that excuse.

Much of Christ's teachings are clearly rooted in the message that He was a human being, just like you and me, a human being who had learned and earned a way to a higher level of existence. One of His most well-known statements is, "Verily, verily I say unto you, the works that I do shall ye do also, and greater works than these shall ye do."[6]

I don't think He was kidding.

He not only gave us full permission to become like Him—a master—but He taught us how to do so and wholly expected that we would.

Those of us who are doing our inner work—who are living in love and harmony as fully as possible, who are resolving our personal dramas quickly, who are persistently applying what we learn every day—those of us who are training our attention to rest with the divine are all, on the road to mastery. Each of us at our own pace, according to our level of commitment and our true motivation, is attaining some level of mastery.

My goal is to invite you, perhaps challenge you, and most definitely to inspire you to choose again. To choose more. To choose from a desire so deep within your soul that the very awareness of it transports you to higher realms. To choose in faith and courage, to fully embrace mastery, to gain absolute clarity, explore, consider, and be present with what being a master means—then choose to make that commitment. Choose to be a part of the critical mass that will bring this planet into the next golden age.

A Call to Mastery

Chapter 2:
GLOBAL PURIFICATION AND THE
NEXT GOLDEN AGE

*As you ascend in the spirit, structured reality falls away
and has no bearing and little relevance to your awareness.
In love and spirit there are neither hierarchies nor struc-
ture. Love is the Source of your life.*

— *Glenda Greene*
Love Without End, Jesus Speaks

We are living in a phase when the energy of the planet is
moving very rapidly toward the next golden age. In fact, the
cycle has already begun. A cosmic movement that is expand-
ing our light for the fulfillment of this divine plan is quicken-
ing us.

There have been several golden ages before. In a golden
age we join the heavenly masters, sharing in their powers and many other natural abilities that we now consider
miracles.

The extreme polarity of good and evil so prevalent in our
world today indicates that we are already in the early stages
of this new cycle. This polarity is a reflection of the mass
purification of mankind. The initial force of purification can
seem pretty horrendous. Detoxification on a global scale just
plain stinks. It can hurt and can make us sick.

In the previous ages of enlightenment we were full masters, beings of great light and power. We fell deeply in love

with our manifestations, our creations and our powers.

The outer world we were able to command into being began commanding us. Our attention, the most important ingredient for creation, moved away from the Source of all that is and became enamored with lesser things. Thus, our radiation, the vibration of our energy, came to be more like our creations and less like our Creator.

The word "sin" as it was originally used in the Aramaic language means to miss the mark.

"If in the quest of things in the outer senses, he becomes so occupied that the conscious attention becomes fixed on the manifestation instead of the Supreme Presence which produces it, then again he has missed the mark."[5]

In the fall of the previous golden ages, we missed the mark, and as we vibrate at the same rate of that upon which we put our attention, we made a vibrational shift. We took on a heavier, denser frequency, thus sinking into the physical realm as physical beings, forfeiting our existence as masters for the time being.[6]

For many centuries we misdirected our attention and allowed our discordant feelings to dominate the quality of our creations. We forgot we were masters and pretended to believe in the illusion of imperfection we formulated. We became satisfied with our limitations, and habituated to the acceptance of the limitations of time and space. Yet, we are still very powerful creators and have created a world of many marvelous and terrible things.

The result of this lapse into forgetfulness of who we really are is the worldwide destructive state from which we are now being purged. For some, it is a very agonizing and frightening purge. For others, it is an opportunity to return mankind to the glory of the golden age and the mastery of this world.

It is crucial to have a large population of people advancing on the road to mastery during this great cleansing and during the birth and infancy of the new cycle.

Let's first look at the purification process on an individual basis to better understand how it works on a global level.

About thirty to fifty feet beyond our bodies, there is an electronic belt or field like a bubble surrounding each of us. Thought-forms (the offspring of attention coupled with emotion) emanate vibrational waves traveling out and accumulating within this electronic field.

This accumulation contains the by-product energy of all of our thought-forms—both positive and negative, that is to say, those thought-forms vibrating at higher frequencies as well as lower frequencies.

The accumulation of human thought, emotion, and desire eventually, or sometimes instantly, ricochets off the electronic belt, bringing back to us the final product—our creations. Sometimes this gathered mass from our consciousness can be held in our field for several lifetimes. Sometimes it will rebound very quickly. Usually we will just receive a steady stream flowing back to us.

One way or another, our energy will find its way home. This is the principle supporting such sayings as, "You reap what you sow," "What goes around, comes around," and "What you give, you receive in like kind."

When we have any inharmonious thoughts or feelings, we inflict disharmony upon our lives and ourselves. When we have love and compassion for others, we are also the recipients of those great gifts every bit as much, or more, as those for whom they are intended.

What happens when we begin putting forth more and more thought-forms of a particular frequency? Let's say we start to think more thoughts and hold greater feelings that vibrate at higher levels. This would change our world dramatically.

For instance, we see this when one initially begins practicing inner work, a spiritual practice or a powerful form of therapy. Often, one finds at first that all hell breaks loose. Our lives appear to fall apart or are bombarded by crises.

Physics tells us two things cannot occupy the same space at the same time. By raising the level of thought form, a person sends waves of higher energy into her electronic belt. As higher energy builds, it literally forces out and replaces the lower frequency energy. That lower energy then shoots back, creating conditions reflecting the lower thought-form from which it came. Thus, the electronic field is being cleansed and purification takes place as the newer, more positive energy replaces the accumulative mass of past negativity.

It may look and feel pretty bad for a while, even painful, as this purification causes turmoil. However, once we are free from these past accumulations, not only is the quality of our lives better than ever before, but we are more likely to reclaim our mastery. (In Part II – The Vehicles, we will look at ways to move through such a process more comfortably.) The key is to maintain the higher vibrations so we don't spend our lives just rotating energy. We have all known people whose lives are a series of dramatic highs and lows.

Devoting ourselves to mastery at this time is vital to individuals as well as to the planet. It takes a master to rise above the past, stay in the present, and expand into the new age. It takes collective mastery to achieve this for all humanity.

The process of individual purification is very much like what we are going through as a planet. Violence, drug addiction, disease—these brands of destruction are crippling us as they cover the globe. We are seeing what mass purification from mass accumulation does to a world whose time has come to face the natural consequences of its own creations.

Centuries of accumulated discord—our discord—are being unleashed. In times of war, for instance, it's pretty easy to become critical, even outraged. We feel and act as if it's all someone else's doing. We speak in terms of "them" or "they." Well, there is no "them" or "they" —only "we." And "we" have created our present situation. Every act of hate, even mild irritation, has gone out into the ethers making its own little deposit. Every time we get angry because someone cut us off on the highway, we make a deposit. Even the tantrum of an unruly child is a contribution. These are the minor ones.

Gather those along with all the major, devastating offenses and, over a period of a few millennia, what we have is a planetary atmosphere personifying toxicity. Words like "responsibility" and "commitment" have become almost profane in a world where freedom has become our object of worship. The truly "dirty" words are the ones like "war," "AIDS" and "heroin." And unless we—each of us—take responsibility for our part in this creation by responding to it through making a choice to attain mastery, in this embodiment, the freedom we worship may fall and shatter like a false idol.

I am not the bearer of bad news. The major networks have a more than adequate handle on that job. And I am not planting seeds of guilt. I am advocating correction; not guilt, but correction. The consciousness movement of the past fifty years or so is a part of that correction. Someone did not just wake up one morning and say, "Okay, peace and love, man." It didn't just happen to catch on as a new fad. Our consciousness has been on a very well planned journey. As we have been moving toward this new cycle, the heavens have been raining light rays of love and compassion upon us, penetrating us with remembrance, awakening us to a clearer recognition of our magnificence as divine beings.

There has been a momentum building—a momentum gaining much force and power, gathering the critical mass necessary to return us to our mastery. Through our free will, we have absorbed and used this immense assistance from the beings of light. We have generated more and more love and compassion. As we generate love, we become love. And the light grows ever more brilliant, replacing the dark.

Thus, the appearance of polarity and duality we now see in our world indicates we have amassed enough light to activate the release of centuries of mankind's accumulated discord.

There are many laws of nature and the law governing this purification, just as all the other laws, is no respecter of persons. Just as the law of gravity does not care who is standing under the apple tree when an apple falls, so, too, the law of purification does not pay heed to who created the mess; if it's your mess it must come back to you. As it does, it can also affect everyone around you, except for those who have mastered their emotional world, to some extent at least.

Saturating our field with high-frequency thought and vibration is resulting in the worldwide eviction of some pretty nasty energy. In the presence of mastery, we can hold the vibration and maintain the harmony necessary to move through and complete this process. Without mastery, the challenge may be too overwhelming. We have been strong enough to ride the wave of light that has brought us this far. Now we are being called upon to become that wave of light, to fulfill the divine plan that will bring us into the golden age as masters.

There is no question about whether this new cycle is our future. By its very nature, the divine plan must be fulfilled. No human hand can interfere with universal law. However, how we arrive at the apex of our destiny is completely up to us. At this critical juncture in our evolution, we can advance into the golden age through mass transcendence or through mass annihilation. The choice is ours.

Chapter 3:
THE THREE LEVELS OF MASTERY

Blessed is the Human Being who practices pure intent in all aspects of his life. For this is the one who will climb the stairs of ascension. This is the one who will see the face of God and it will turn out to be his own!

— Kryon
A New Dispensation

Mastery is a very broad term and within it are several connotations and layers. For our purposes, let's consider three types, or degrees, of spiritual mastery, keeping in mind that within each category there are several layers of proficiency.

1. Master in the Making
2. Full Mastery
3. Ascended Master

Throughout this book, I will often use the blanket term "master" to refer to any or all of these levels.

The Master in the Making

Masters in the making are people whose awareness of their own thoughts and feelings are exceptionally keen. They have an in-depth comprehension of the power and effects of attention, emotion and visualization and do their best to live according to that understanding. They manage their energy well and are able to "flow" energy (give and receive) easily and at will. The master in the making knows the physical

31

body is a temple of God and Goddess and treats it as such.

• They maintain a higher-than-average vibrational frequency through conscious application of whatever practice(s) work for them. They stick with what works, becoming more proficient and creating a momentum. While they consider and sometimes integrate new teachings, they do not succumb to the endless onslaught of choices, becoming a "jack-of-all-trades" and "master of none." They know one of the surest ways to limit expansion in the light is to run from one sensational thing to another, seeking the sense and ego gratification of supernatural phenomena and human approval.

• They are discerning. They use their discernment when choosing an outside source for assistance, such as an energy worker, body worker or therapist. They are humble and seek such assistance when appropriate.

• They recognize that consciousness is all there is and they maintain a consciousness that embraces their oneness with the divine. They know they are one with God and Goddess and, therefore, they are God and Goddess, limited only by their own doubts.

• They are peacefully detached and not easily controlled by their emotions. They do not need drama in order to feel alive. They love mastery and intentionally call it forth, through thought, word and deed.

• They are beginning to manifest everyday miracles in this phase, such as healing, creating synchronistic events through use of the spoken word (prayer) and visualizations, and controlling some aspects of nature. These miracles reflect the degree of belief the master in the making has at any particular point while on the road to mastery. As each miracle manifests, it provides proof and builds confidence, helping the master in the making realize they can control their manifestations to a greater degree.

• They are alert to the tug and pull of the sensory appetites and willfully surrender them to their God presence for healthy management.

• They precipitate spontaneous healings, although they may not always be aware of them. The master in the making can shift the perception of those in his presence. A change of mind is often all that is needed to heal a condition. Because of the vibrational frequency the master in the making radiates, others in their presence may be raised to a higher frequency, enabling them to rise above the problem and be released from it, or reach a resolution. One of Einstein's better-known quotes gives a dimension of understanding to this concept: "A problem cannot be solved at the same level of mind at which it was created."

• The master in the making recognizes we can't really own or possess much of anything because everything belongs to God, and since we are one with Him, it all belongs to us, too. Possessiveness is a fear unfamiliar to the master in the making.

• The master in the making frequently, perhaps several times daily, invokes assistance from the divine beings and angelic host. They receive the help for which they call, for they have come to expect it and accept it.

• The masters in the making are, for the most part, living in the present. They are not lingering in or reliving the past nor anxiously anticipating the future. In his book *The Power of Now*, Eckhart Tolle masterfully explains the art of being present. The popularity of this book indicates that mastery is a subject we are ready to embrace because *The Power of Now* is essentially about mastery.

• Masters in the making are comfortable with financial concerns because they are free from the misconceptions of duality and the experiences such thoughts create. They invest in oneness. They don't experience separation from their supply because they don't experience separation from the source of that supply.

• The master in the making must be reminded occasionally to engage tacitly in this world. "To be in the world but not of it" is the idea. But the challenge at this point is the "being in it" part, not the "not being of it" part. The things, relationships and illusions of this world can begin to lose their appeal. What others perceive to be important or fun or desirable, the master in the making may find insignificant and maybe even frivolous. When, through the dynamic focus of attention, we begin to play and worship in other worlds, in the worlds of the gods and goddesses, this life can become a bit lusterless. So the master in the making is mindful to keep at least one foot firmly planted in the stuff of this world that supports love and joy, offers passion, and holds his or her interest—even if they have to fake it every once in a while.

• Masters in the making don't have many problems in their lives. They don't need them or want them, so they don't create them.

• They forgive easily, but seldom need to.

• They are generous and give freely and fearlessly.

• They place a high priority on emotional balance and their vibration allows for a feeling world settled into a natural centeredness.

• They have an understanding and respect for the universal laws. These laws are impersonal and the master in the making is not prone to the entitlement issues that can fool us into thinking we are special enough to be exempt from the effects of these laws.

• The master in the making is learning to surrender unconditionally to divine will. In so doing, personal will merges more and more with divine will.

• They are divinely protected and call forth that protection on a regular basis.

• The road to mastery, like the road to San Tiago in Paul

Coelho's book *The Pilgrimage,* is for the "common people."[7] Mastery is available to anyone and everyone who seeks it and reaches for it.

• Often masters in the making seem just like everyone else because, in truth, they are just like anyone else. They may not be easy to spot. They are not busy convincing everyone they are powerful, nor do they need to perform for approval. A flower doesn't have to yell out, "Look at me, see how beautiful I am!" Margaret Thatcher said it perfectly: "Being powerful is like being a lady; if you have to tell people you are, you aren't."

You may find the master in the making possessing just a few of these attributes, several of them or all of them at any given time. This would depend on how much accumulated goodness they have brought forth with them from past embodiments, how far along on the road to mastery they are in this embodiment, how much they rely on the ascended masters and angels and how much they devote their attention to the divine.

They work at keeping their vibrations pure and strong, their attention focused on their God-presence and their heart filled with unconditional divine love. They have to work at all of this, through conscious effort, because they are still human. They are kind and gentle with themselves and others in remembering we are all still human. The master in the making is the apprentice who is learning, practicing and developing with the intention to expand into the next light ray—that of full mastery.

Full Mastery

We don't need to come into this cycle of mastery in order to attain ascension. However, it is a very desirable state of being and the master in the making may very well choose to

35

reach this level of service to the light. It is here we can give the greatest assistance to all of humanity, for miracles abound here. Full mastery is the transcendence of human emotion, desire, chaos, discord, and distress, as well as physical limitation or decay of any kind.

These beings have come to the pinnacle of existence in this octave and taken command. They have purified their bodies, minds and hearts to such an extent they are clear vessels of pure divine light. In other words, their vibratory action is at such a high, fast rate of movement they are not governed by normal functioning. They are not easily subject to the consequences of our human creations.

These masters, through the power of their love, can instantly precipitate anything they choose from the universal divine substance. They transport through time and space at will. They are able to be in more than one place at a time. They can affect events anywhere in the world through the power of their attention and intention.

They are in a position to be of great help to us all because of the strength and effect of their radiation. They are healers and catalysts. They often work together with the ascended masters to protect us and orchestrate activities beyond our awareness. Sometimes, we struggle to understand circumstances that make no sense to us. At those times, it's most helpful to remember we do not always know the whole story.

We cannot always accept the appearance of things. We don't always see the big picture; our perception is limited and unable to take in the full scope of divine will and activity. We do not know when one of the masters may have saved us from disaster or manipulated the flow of events to bring us to an achievement. It is very difficult to recognize a full master unless she chooses to reveal herself, which is usually for a purpose that fulfills the divine plan.

One of the major differences between the full master and the ascended master is that the ascended master is no longer in a human body and cannot experience imperfection to any degree.

The Ascended Master

In India they are known as gods or deities. The Catholics call them Saints. The "I Am" Activity refers to them as ascended masters. These great beings, in the past, have walked the Earth in human form, just like you and I do now. They have experienced struggle and known physical pleasure. They have freed themselves from both. Through purification and love, they have reached a vibrational action that loosens the Earth's gravitational hold on them. They literally become beings of light and rise beyond this octave into the octaves of the heavens. These divine beings still possess bodies. They are not physical bodies, but bodies of light. They can and do appear at will in a visible form in this dimension, when the divine plan calls for it.

The ascended masters experience only perfection, joy, wisdom and power. They are unable to suffer or struggle in any way. They cannot be tempted nor can they make a mistake. Thousands of people have risen to this status. Among these, one ascension, thus far, has taken place publicly, imbedding its importance into our consciousness for centuries—the ascension of Jesus Christ.

If we look at Jesus' time on Earth, we see all phases of mastery played out. He began as a master in the making, very much a human being who was passionately learning and seeking knowledge of the truth. He expanded into full mastery with miracles abounding, transcending his humanness. Finally, through His ascension, He became an ascended master, leaving us with the record of this activity so we may take up His momentum and reach the ascension through our own mastery.

Chapter 4:
SEX & SILLY PUTTY

Pleasure is a freedom-song,
But it is not freedom.
It is the blossoming of your desires,
But it is not their fruit.
It is a depth calling unto a height
But it is not the deep nor the high.
It is the caged taking wing,
But it is not space encompassed.
Ay, in very truth, pleasure is a freedom-song.
And I fain would have you sing it with
fullness of heart; yet I would not have you
lose your hearts in the singing.

— *Kahlil Gibran*
The Prophet

If you ever played with Silly Putty as a kid, you probably remember the way that stuff could miraculously pick up pictures from newsprint, especially the funnies. Recently, while doing laundry by hand (I *am* in the jungle), I saw for a split second a print in the wet clothes, which triggered an intense, cellular memory of Silly Putty. All my senses, suddenly and in unison, fully transported me to the joys of that unique substance. Right then, my memory banks flew open and what tumbled out was a celebratory, sensory resurrection of my long-ago Silly Putty delights.

I could feel its smooth surface and how it would mold to the creases and tiny wrinkles in my hands. I smelled that earthy yet synthetic scent. I saw the pink/beige blandness merge with the innocence of Li'l Abner. I heard the intimate creak of that plastic egg and felt the delicious anticipation of hours spent in play, fun, and pleasure.

Boy, did I ever love Silly Putty!

Then one fleeting thought extinguished the entire déjà-vu moment. I felt myself float up to the surface of the present, back from the depths of memory, keeping with me the barest tinge of that Silly-Putty ecstasy. A thought snapped me back to the here and now, a simple and natural progression in the experience. It was something like, "Maybe I can find some here in Suriname. Maybe someone can send me some from home."

What registered in my then "back-to-laundry" mind was I had outgrown the stuff. I didn't really want it anymore. I could be temporarily tempted by my senses, but Silly Putty and the activities surrounding it no longer vibrated at a rate that could hold my attention for very long. I knew if I did get some, it would keep my interest only briefly. The experience would quickly pale and fall short of what had once brought such uninhibited enjoyment. This detachment was just a part of growing up.

So why is "Sex and Silly Putty" the name of this chapter? You may not want to know. For some people, sex is one of those things they simply outgrow once they are far along on the road to mastery. They leave it behind as they pick up other things in greater allegiance with their intentions. At some point, they will make the deliberate choice to detach from sexual activity or will almost imperceptibly just grow beyond it, except of course for providing a loving means of transportation for incoming souls. For the time being, we still procreate in the same old way. However, sooner or later, for some who are dedicated to mastery, sexual activity inevitably makes an exit, at least for a while.

Expansion into true mastery frees us from most of the physical, sensory desires that come with human experience, including sex. Sometimes this happens gradually over time, and we hardly notice them fading away; the desires simply disappear in the brilliance of our new, higher radiance. Sometimes we choose to deliberately cause this to happen using the skills we have so far acquired, as masters in the making, to transcend and therefore outgrow the vibration of sexual longing.

Masters throughout the centuries have taught that expending life force energy through sexual activity can distract, obstruct and indefinitely delay the progress of those on the road to mastery. This is absolutely not in any way, shape or form about giving up, sacrificing or repressing anything. This is about radiating at a frequency that no longer holds desire for sex or many other indulgences of the senses. When we truly don't want something, it's not hard or sacrificial to let it go; once it's really gone, we don't miss it anymore. Sometimes our memories can fool us into thinking we miss it for a bit, but that doesn't last long. The vibrational frequency of the master is unable to hold that energy for long.

In mastery we literally rise above the sexual drive that can keep us anchored within the density of the physical realm. For many, this is a difficult choice; it is an important fork in the road to mastery.

One direction leads us to a process that usually takes time. It requires we be patient and gentle with ourselves, yet strong and vigilant. It is here so many of us waver from our intended destination. We often choose the other direction instead—the one that promises more familiar ground, but that can keep us from the higher ground for many lifetimes.

Learning to genuinely redirect this potent energy for use

in achieving mastery is in itself a precious lesson. When we reach the point on our journey where we can manipulate such vital energy at will, we will know we have advanced on our way to mastery.

I would like to take a short detour here and address a prevalent concern.

Many people view abstinence as a serious threat to their balance. They want no extremes, and take the middle road in all things. Yes, being centered and balanced can open us to perfection. However, the question I must ask in regard to this concern is: "How can we lose something we don't even have? Like balance?"

Look around. Look inside. Listen for a while.

We swim in an ocean of extreme behavior. The most widely heard songs are about sex, drugs and violence. Our most popular movies are about sex, drugs and violence. Our ecology is quickly metamorphosing into the shadow projections of our psychology. Obesity, diabetes and HIV/AIDS are growing exponentially. We are engaging in a war that is killing of thousands of human beings. We are spending more money on plastic surgery, less time with our children and little energy healing the consequences of our choices.

And we should worry about losing our balance? What balance? We should be concerned about "going over the edge" if we are more devoted to reclaiming our divinity than we are to getting laid?

I think not.

Human sexuality is a complex arena, filled with emotional, psychological and genetic components.

I am not an authority on the subject. My point of reference comes from experience, professionally as a Rapid Eye Technician[8] and personally as a woman. (For information on RET, see My Story.)

Professionally, I found some of my clients had low-functioning libidos. Sex held little or no interest for them. I also saw clients for whom sex was fairly important. For various reasons, some of these people experienced their sexuality from the perception of guilt and shame.

Guilt and shame calibrate at the lowest end of the vibrational scale as stated in Dr. Hawkins' book *Power vs. Force.*[9] These emotions have a dense, heavy vibration, keeping us trapped in the physical realm and in our own misery. For these people, there is a prevalent tendency to suppress or repress their sexual energy. This is not the way to approach mastery. To just suddenly say, "Okay, I'm becoming a master so no more sex for me in thought or word or deed," could result in a huge stifling of our true feelings and result in a counterproductive backfire.

Sheer willpower alone is not the recommended method. Stifling such a volatile energy is dangerous and unhealthy. That energy must have expression until it is transcended. If it is crammed into a box of guilt and shame, it will find some way out, otherwise it can cause great imbalance. Anything from depression to perversion and addiction or violence can be the result. In the extreme, our world is reflecting this dysfunction back to us through such abominations as rape and the well-publicized pedophilia among the Catholic clergy. The shadow side of the sexual self lurks, hoping for a way to gain control. Nothing in these human creations is in allegiance with attaining mastery.

On the other end of the vibrational spectrum, we find those who are blessed with a truly healthy ability to embrace and express their sexuality. These people are what I like to call the "love makers." When all of our chakras (see Part I, Chapter 5), the higher ones as well as the lower, are fully engaged and completely open in the giving and receiving of the deepest parts of our selves, when we unravel from the inside out and surrender without limit to the ecstasy of oneness, when there is a blissful and total absence of any judgment or fear or smallness, then we are literally in the process of making love.

It's easy to imagine the angels showing up on such occasions, rejoicing in the love being created, gathering that love and carrying it out into the world as a gift of light. Truly such making of love is an outpouring of a radiation that heals, prospers, and uplifts. Nevertheless, it is still bound by the constraints of the human physical experience. It is limited in its ability to bless all of mankind.

Those who vibrate at this level are fairly close to shedding their sexual attachments, even though those attachments can be big. They are releasing their reliance on sex as a means of expressing their light. They are coming to realize if they choose mastery, the magnitude of their love and light will expand beyond measure. They see they have been trying to run infinite power through a very finite vessel.

This is not to say that mastery can only be achieved by those who chose celibacy. However, celibacy offers an opportunity to experience the emergence of a consciousness that literally embodies a state of oneness with the divine. It can be a "jump start" for anyone traveling the road to mastery who wishes to truly offer himself to God and Goddess in mind, spirit, and body.

In mastery, the energy once directed by sexual activity is redirected into higher realms and recycled into light rays for the blessing of humanity. This energy is also held in its pure form within the individual's electronic field for use in achieving the ascension.

Ascended masters are not limited in the making of love by the burdensome, earthly vibrations of the physical body. Rather, they radiate a supreme quality of creative power in unlimited quantities. They are completely free of any desire that might trap them in the addictive needs and wants to which human beings are so susceptible.

No matter where on the vibrational spectrum you may be at this moment, the step from human sexual activity to masterful transcendence begins by asking. Remember the answer is always ask, demand, command, and expect the natural unfolding of the assistance you require, as any master would. (In Part II, we will discuss commanding and other techniques in detail.)

My personal experience has revealed that the quality of our motivation is a vital factor in determining the quality of our relationship with the divine. On two separate occasions I have felt a very distinct, unexpected shift occur in my sexual energy.

The first was in the late 1980s. I was twenty-nine or thirty years old and the shift occurred within hours of being introduced to Sahaja Yoga. The second was a few years ago, shortly after I discovered the "I Am" Activity of Saint Germain (for information about both these practices, see My Story). In both instances, I knew with certain clarity, that each spiritual practice was exactly what was in divine order for me then. They had my name on them and I wanted them with all my heart and soul. With each one, I devoted my entire self and was motivated only by the desire to love and serve God and Goddess and raise my vibrational state.

Looking back, I realize it must have been purity of motivation and devotion that quickly lifted me beyond the demands of my libido. It was as if I had stepped up onto sacred ground and in so doing shed, at least for a while, that part of myself. It was like getting a sign-on bonus—a bonus that kept me focused on my newly found practices until I was fully and safely enveloped in them. After a few months, it was as if I had gained the needed strength to deal with the human aspects of myself again, because they did reappear.

It is a kind of dance we do with our higher selves and

our human desires. Sometimes one leads, then the other. If we are consistent in training and managing our attention and if our motive is pure and strong, it usually doesn't take very long for the higher self to be leading most of the time. It's when our egos and appetites nudge their way in and take the lead that we must stay most aware and be deliberate in our choices.

I speak, of course, in terms of all thoughts, words and actions vibrating at a lower frequency, not only those of a sexual nature. The more experience we have with this dance, the stronger becomes our consciousness and our ability to take command of the lead. Relying on divine assistance and shifting our attention, if our intention is sincere, will almost always take us back to our higher selves.

However, when they don't, then what? That is when we consider the delicate balance between repressing and transcending. There may be those times, especially early on in attaining mastery, when we feel the healthiest choice at the moment is to honor the human and grant its wish. I had a teacher once who said in regard to this, "If you really must, throw the dog a bone once in awhile."

After making such a choice, you may experience a change in vibration. It may feel as if the great masters or angels have moved away from you; maybe they have turned away. Never. They don't leave us; we leave them. These beings are not subject to concern about human behavior. They live according to the laws of the universe. It is the law of vibration that may cause a sense of abandonment in you, not any judgment or retribution on the part of the divine.

When "we take a dive," so to speak, our vibration lowers and we no longer function at a rate allowable for the visceral connection with the divine previously present when our vibrations were higher. Some teachings refer to a veil between this dimension and higher realms. That veil thins when we vibrate high and pure, allowing us to be in touch with the activity in the other octaves. The veil thickens when we have a drop in vibrations, causing us to feel distant from those realms and more enmeshed in this one. Obviously, overindulging any of our senses for too long will cause a thickening of the veil.

At these times it is important we do not allow ourselves to plunge further on the vibrational scale by generating guilt and fear. Remember this is not about judgment. It is about vibration. You can do much damage by taking on guilt over what you have done or fear that you have "sinned" and may never get back.

Quite to the contrary, this would be the time to humbly, yet squarely, face your higher presence and the cosmic beings and make your call, perform your practices, call on the law of forgiveness, pray, talk, or whatever you do to keep your attention focused on the divine. Soon your divine presence will take the lead again and you will begin to feel reunited with God and the beings of light. This does not mean anytime we want to its okay to overindulge in lower vibratory activities. We can't go there and then just come right back to the privileges of mastery.

It doesn't work that way.

First, the more often we lower our frequency and the longer we stay there, the heavier our vibrations become and the more difficult it is to raise them again. The human gets used to leading—it loves the music, and the music can seduce us into forgetting that our mastery is far more rewarding and gratifying. That is, until the quality of life begins to crumble and erode. Then we remember again and run back to God—for a while. Throw the dog that bone more often than you absolutely must and soon the dog will be dining on your hand!

Second, there is an element of grace involved here. Your

higher presence and the divine beings know absolutely, clearly, at all times, what is in your heart.

If we attempt to manipulate the law of vibration, it will backfire. We cannot indiscriminately feed our appetites and expect to achieve mastery at the same time. The entire concept is a contradiction. Just as in the fall of the golden ages, such an attempt would withdraw us from the presence of perfection and bind us to the vibration of the Earth.

However, if our motivation is pure and we are not fooling ourselves, if we make our choices from a heart that truly desires to do only divine will, then the heavens will read our hearts and gladly help us to rise again into the higher states. Here is the bottom line:

This is a process. At first, we take a few steps forward and then a few steps back until we don't anymore.

Is it sometimes difficult?

Yes.

Does it sometimes take effort and self-discipline?

Yes.

Is it worth it?

Only you can answer that.

Is becoming a Christ worth it? Is the mastery of life worth it to you?

Sexuality is a personal matter. So is one's mastery. They are both personal because they are directed solely through free will. No one has the right to dictate how or what we choose in regard to the use of our life stream and life force energy, not even God. We are free to choose. Our destiny lies in that freedom.

Not everyone will hunger for his or her mastery and ascension in this lifetime or perhaps not for several yet to come. Not everyone will choose to be of a consciousness compelling them to move beyond sexuality and the many other all-consuming demands of the senses. For these many people, one of my greatest wishes is that they develop a relationship with this part of themselves that takes on the role of play.

The first book in a series, *Conversations with God,* by Neale Donald Walsch, contains a simple and wonderful section on this subject as God says:

"Play with sex. Play with it. It's just about the most fun you can have with your body, if you're talking of strictly physical experiences alone. But for goodness sake, don't destroy sexual innocence and pleasure and the purity of the fun, the joy, by misusing sex. Don't use it for power or hidden purpose other than the purest joy and the highest ecstasy, given and shared—which is new life! Have I not shown a delicious way to make more of you? With regard to denial, I have dealt with that before. Nothing holy has ever been achieved through denial. Yet desires change as even larger realities are glimpsed. It is not unusual therefore, for people to simply desire less, or even no sexual activity—or, for that matter, any of a number of activities of the body. For some the activities of the soul become foremost—and by far the most pleasurable."[10]

To move about freely and innocently within the borders of our sensory experience can serve as a means to an end. Sex without guilt and shame can foster a vibratory environment both receptive and conducive to the eventual dissipation of the attachment to sex. When we are comfortably at peace with any aspect of ourselves, we are safe to detach from it if we so choose. If enough people gain the balanced, healthy perception of sex as a gift for our play, they can contribute to the upliftment of the mass consciousness that is so plugged into the glorification of sex and its deviance.

Experiencing this kind of sex may, for some people, actually be an important part of their spiritual journey. Nonetheless, sex alone is not a substitute for achieving mastery.

Using life force energy for sex, especially at lower levels of consciousness can cause us to get stuck and prevent the expansion into mastery and the ascension.

As I stated earlier, for many people, such attainment is not the goal at this time. For these people, Walsch's enlightened words are a great gift to be integrated and shared. However, within the experience of childlike playfulness is the potential to "grow up." The mastery of life is the fulfillment of that potential as divine beings.

We have become very skilled at honoring, embracing, and revering our humanness. Being a human being is a glorious and wonderful gift. It is one of the vehicles through which the divine expresses itself. We have had centuries of enjoying both the beauty of our humanness and the suffering of our humanness. We are now being beckoned to rise into a beauty unimaginable by the human mind and to live in a state where suffering cannot exist.

It is time we graduate. We are done here as human beings. We are on the threshold of our mastery. As divine beings, grown to full stature, we leave behind those lesser things of our youth.

Like sex and Silly Putty.

The Many Faces of God and Goddess

I feel compelled to honor my present truth and share some changes I have experienced and some lessons I have learned since first writing this book a couple of years ago. I have come to understand there are many faces of God and Goddess, and the more of them we can see and serve, the more richly crafted our lives become.

From within the current spiritual renaissance there have emerged what appear to be two fundamentally different theologies. I have heard them offhandedly referred to as the "ascenders" and the "descenders." The ascenders' view has already been explained in this chapter, to some extent. Of course, there are those who would be more or less severe in their interpretation of the necessity to transcend the physical body in order to "reach heaven."

The descenders hold as their truth the pre-Christian understanding that life-force energy is sexual and instinctual in nature. The physical/material world is not considered something to combat, overcome, withdraw from, or transcend. Fully and responsibly embracing it is what actually leads to the transcendence we seek. Life-force energy is a part of divine power governing life on our planet in all its abundance. This ancient theology conveys respect and reverence for these forces that reside at the core of our being.

Duality and separation cease to have an avenue for expression in this belief system. We are not placed in these bodies for the sole purpose of rejecting them so we can go back to living a "higher" life without them. We have "descended" so that we could take these bodies and come to Earth for the purpose of experiencing and expressing divinity through an organic, full, healthy, rich, and holistic existence.

In this school of thought, literally *everything* is divine—we do not separate (and thus fall prey to the illusion of duality) our bodies from our souls, our desires from our spirit. We are wholly divine—that includes these vessels that allow us to exalt the human experience. Of course, here, too, it's all about vibration. When we use and direct our divine power of sexuality, physicality, and expansion of the senses in responsible ways, our vibrations can soar and aid in raising the consciousness of the entire planet.

As a species we have so far for the most part been unable to successfully integrate all aspects of our humanness. On one end of the scale many have denied, stifled, or repressed, which has led inevitably to a swing to the other side of overindulgence, obsession, and exploitation.

The Celtic word for sacred life force is *nwyfre.*

"... to come to know and accept Nwyfre in all its power into your being, without becoming obsessed by it and without using it exploitively. We learn that the powers of Nwyfre that create children and animals, plants and trees, that nourish them with the energy they need to create wealth and beauty on Earth, can flow freely and powerfully through them once they accept their destiny as conscious moral beings on Earth. The time of denying responsibility is over. Nwyfre calls us to awake, and in doing so offers us potential for both abundance and liberation as we accept responsibility for our life and the way we live it."[11]

My personal experience in the last year has shown me the glory of accepting as truth all aspects of God and Goddess within me, not just some of them, but all of them, including full appreciation of this miraculous body and what I have come to call "cosmic lovemaking." During the original writing of this book I had been celibate for several glorious years. I sincerely support anyone who chooses that path for whatever duration of time best suits them. Celibacy offers a very effective and intimate way to stretch our awareness of the physical and the spiritual world. Due to the blessings of celibacy, when the time came, I was able to re-embrace the nonduality of those two worlds and live a life representative of the wholeness of all creation. I now do my best to consciously stay within a balance of these different theologies, honoring the divine gifts both have to offer.

The Divine Blueprint

I recently had a dream that says much about our romantic relationships and the search for the perfect mate. I was sitting at a small table speaking to someone unseen. As I spoke, my right elbow rested on the table and my hand was open with the fingers slightly spread. I was talking about the divine blueprint.

We go through life, sometimes desperately, searching for that person who will "fit" us just perfectly. We seek that piece that will complete us. However, every time a hand is placed up against ours in the hope of a flawless fit, the fingers inevitably slip through and we end up grasping one another rather than making a perfect match. In such a grasp we may find security and whatever the human self needs at the time, yet complete wholeness, perfect fullness and satisfaction will, after time, still elude us. Those of us who have the good fortune to be blessed with an enchanted love, a divine union bringing us closer to God and Goddess, have but a glimpse of the sacred state that comes from completing the divine blueprint.

The only hand that will fit, the only piece able to make our blueprint whole, the thing for which we hunger so deeply, yet oftentimes unknowingly, is divine self. We continue to seek, hope, and expect the perfect human relationship capable of satisfying that hunger.

There is no such thing. No matter how exciting our earthly relationships are, no matter how good it gets, the soul continues to thirst for the ecstasy of God's union with Himself through us. When we allow that union to take place, we experience ourselves as one and inseparable from God. The divine blueprint is then whole and in its proper place within the grid of our individual existence. In *Everyday Grace*, Marianne Williamson says it with eloquence:

"You will know that to God you are everything, when He has become everything to you."[12]

Chapter 5:
THE CHAKRA SYSTEM

If you are really sons and daughters of God, it is time for you to claim the fullness of what that means. The Divine does not want the worst for you or even the mediocre. It wants the best.

— Bartholomew
Reflections of an Elder Brother

Some understanding of the chakra system is fundamental to the practice of mastery, especially in terms of training and managing our attention. Chakras are wheel-like energy centers that surround and are located throughout the body. They govern and influence specific functions on all four levels—physically, emotionally, mentally, and spiritually. Caroline Myss is a well-known spiritual author and public speaker. Her book *Anatomy of the Spirit* is an excellent source for in-depth learning about the chakra system. Sahaja Yoga (see About the Author, My Story) is also a valuable source because its work with the Kundalini (a divine energy residing in the sacral bone that, once awakened, strengthens our connection to God) is based on the chakra system.

The body can serve as a vessel through which we experience spiritual ecstasy. Intimate relationship with the chakras can bring depth of knowledge, comfort, and appreciation for the body as a sacred instrument. Working with this instrument, learning and loving its gifts, and fine-tuning the chakras can lead to spiritual ecstasy and excellence.

Ancient Eastern teachings have told us there are seven main chakras within the chakra system and several minor ones. In Rapid Eye Technology, we work with twelve chakras, considering them all to be of equal importance. As I mentioned earlier, we have upper and lower chakras, which are not separate, independent bodies. They work interdependently in an intricate weave of energy. The lower chakras are below the waist and influence how we relate to the physical world. They can determine to what degree we stay grounded and integrated with our surroundings. They govern our survival and the quality of that survival.

The following is a list and very abridged description of the chakra system from the ground up:

The tenth chakra, located about twelve inches into the Earth, below our feet, holds our individual space within and upon the Earth.

The first chakra, located at the base of the spine, provides a base for the rest of the chakra system and allows for innocence, purity, and connection to the material world, and governs some aspects of sexuality.

The second chakra, located in the lower abdominal region, orchestrates the flow of creative energy as it shows up on the physical plane, including sexuality, money, power and the reproductive system.

The third chakra, located at the solar plexus (the upper abdominal region), bridges our higher and lower regions. This center holds our personal power and challenges us to be who we really are in spite of any external influence.

Now we move into the upper or higher chakra system. Here, we are provided with a forum for our spiritual evolution and relationship with the divine.

The fourth chakra, located at the heart, primarily handles our feelings and the energy within our emotional field.

The fifth chakra, located at the throat, governs our ability to express, verbally and otherwise, and influences the quality of our voice.

The sixth chakra, located in the forehead, is the focus of our mental and intuitive powers.

The seventh thru ninth chakras, located at the crown of the head and above, direct our ultimate union with God and all that is divine.

The eleventh and twelfth chakras, located in our hands and feet, and immediately surrounding our bodies, oversee some of our healing powers as well as the quality of our auric field.

Generally speaking, when working with this system the goal is to first learn about the chakras. Then develop your sensitivity, allowing physical and intuitive awareness of the activity within these centers. The idea is to cultivate a relationship with these inner aspects of ourselves so we can clear them of negative information, while also opening and strengthening them.

Many people practice some form of energy work, meditation and visualization to connect with these chakras. The desired outcome is to create and maintain a well-balanced chakra system that contributes positively on all levels to our overall well-being. Ultimately, having a very highly functioning chakra system serves as a vital and necessary vehicle for those who are moving forward on the road to mastery.

As masters in the making, the attention must rest mainly on the higher chakras and the aspects associated with them. By doing so we generate a magnetic pull, taking us from the lesser things to the greater things, from the earth to the heavens. We engage in our mastery most profoundly through these higher chakras. It is here we access our divine presence. The higher chakras, when developed, can supply us with such limitless power our intention alone can keep them harmonized. But because this is a holistic, interconnected system, it is vital to honor and maintain health in the lower centers as well as in the higher ones.

My experience has shown that most of us who are serious about wanting to attain our mastery already have a fairly healthy chakra system. If not, then you can claim your place as creator—focus your attention, ask, call forth, command and do the exercises recommended here and in other books as well. (Donna Eden's *Energy Medicine* is a good source for exercises and practices to clear and strengthen the chakras.) Then expect and accept a positive shift in your chakras and your life.

One of my favorite modes for giving the chakras a good tune-up, especially the lower ones, begins with sitting on the ground. Taking a few moments to still the mind, I place my hands, palm down, reverently on Mother Earth, and ask Her to take from me all negativity, whether it is someone else's or mine. (We do take on and carry around other people's energy—until we don't anymore.) Then I see and feel the bottom of my body open up and release itself as Mother Earth literally and lovingly vacuums out the blocks and unwanted energy She may find there. The lower chakras are particularly responsive to the powers of Earth because they govern our earthly existence. As Mother Earth, in all Her compassion, absorbs what I often see in my mind's eye as gooey black stuff, I can feel a great draining away of that heaviness. This flowing forth feels absolutely heavenly as I am cleansed from below and refueled by light from above. Try it sometime. It can be a great contribution to any maintenance program.

Sitting on the Earth, expressing our appreciation to Mother Earth and all She gives and takes from us, will absorb heavy negative energy from the lower chakras.

The four elements—air, water, earth and fire—can play

an important role in the cleansing and strengthening of our chakra system. Sahaja Yoga teaches us that looking into the sky for a few minutes and acknowledging the deities who govern the air will help clear the upper chakras—our heart, throat and head.

Water purifies the left side of our body and the chakras located there. The left side is the female side and governs our emotional body. Soaking our feet and bodies in water, performing rituals involving water and praying to the beings of this element will help to bring and keep our left side in balance.

The right side is our male side; it governs physical action. Fire is the powerful element that clears and fortifies the right side of the body and the chakras affecting it. Looking into fire, using fire with reverence and acknowledging the beings of this element will bless us with a dynamic energy in our physical activity.

Remembering the beings of the elements with love and respect can contribute much to developing a rich, vital chakra system.

The Heart Chakra

The heart chakra yearns for our attention. It is the home of our emotional body. Within the heart lies the sacred authority to channel the Light and Love that is our divinity. To focus and project divine love through the heart to any person or circumstance is one of the greatest activities available to us. Love is not emotion; Love is ability. The degree to which we can generate Love in this way is boundless, and the further along we move in the attainment of mastery, the more mighty this projection can become.

The heart chakra can hear the voice of God speaking within each of us. When we are quiet enough and are in tune enough to hear that voice, a great trust and peace can arise.

When we hear the voice of God speak through our hearts, we no longer judge, doubt, fear or question our feelings. Our hearts then become truly dependable. We can then trust our feelings and begin to know with an unshakable know-ingness.

The emotion of love, which always contains an element of attachment, transforms through the heart into the power of love, which always contains an element of divine consciousness.

This sacred center can send light outward into the world to bless your loved ones, your work, your finances and all of mankind, if you wish. It can act like a huge spotlight, enfolding everything in its path with a love that heals and enlightens. Through visualizations, meditation, prayer, and decree work (explained in Chapter 7) we can connect the heart through the throat center, with the center in the forehead, which then connects to the chakras above the head. In this way, we create a continuous flow of light from our divine presence above us, down through the upper chakras, out through the heart, and then back again to the heavens. Each time we intentionally fuel this circular flow, it grows stronger and ever more far reaching.

The Throat Chakra

The throat chakra acts as a gateway between the heart and the head. It is essential this center be as clean and strong as possible so light may flow freely between those two chakras. The throat chakra finds its mastery in the speaking of truth, in the sweetness of expressing love, and in the absence of excessive, frivolous or aggressive speech.

The meaning and importance of this chakra was immortalized through the ministry of Jesus. He taught the truth known as divine law, His voice being empowered by a pure fifth chakra, carried over great distances as He did so. He did not engage in meaningless small talk and He did not allow fear to stifle the expression of His personal truth and feelings. He was and is the expression of truth.

This chakra is also helpful in exposing and thus expelling negative energy. Negativity loves to hide; it gains power from secrecy, which is why secrets can make us sick. Often, just by verbally naming, disclosing or identifying a problem or issue, it will vanish . The trick is to not give into the temptation to continue talking about the problem. Giving it prolonged attention will reinstate the negativity and defeat the purpose. Simply identify it, expose it, release it and move on.

The throat chakra is of vast importance. Treating it with tender, loving care and being mindful of what we say and what we don't say is a wise practice for those of us who wish to gain mastery.

The Sixth Chakra

Don't think about spaghetti.

So, which mental picture is making your mouth water right now—fettuccini Alfredo or traditional red sauce with meatballs?

The sixth chakra has great influence on our thoughts and images. Controlling the attention is determined much more by what we do think about than by what we don't think about. Telling yourself not to think about anything from which you are seeking freedom, is about as effective as telling yourself not to think about spaghetti.

When thoughts, which are immediately followed by feelings, begin to lead in a direction contradicting your master plan, don't resist. Simply muster up the strength to focus attention on something else. Anything else will do—it doesn't have to be something lofty. Just make it something different—something that makes you feel good, and is perhaps just a notch or two higher on the vibrational scale. This will work well enough to shift your energy up again.

A variation of this pivoting technique is to rely on your sixth chakra to help you reach for a thought that feels better about the same subject. Rather then switching thoughts to something else altogether, you remain focused on the same thing, except you come up with positive thoughts, leading to other positive thoughts.

For instance, a store clerk is rude or does not meet your expectation of good customer service. You find yourself becoming annoyed or offended. Your sixth chakra empowers you to switch your thoughts from angry ones to something that may sound like this: "He must be having a hard day. Dealing with so many demanding people must be very trying. Perhaps he arrived at work late due to all the traffic we've been having lately and he began his day under stress and pressure. Maybe an understanding smile or appreciative word from me could help him out a bit." And so on.

You'll see this pivoting not only releases you from disharmonious thoughts and feelings, but can spill over to uplift others as well. And in so doing, you are using the law of attraction to bring to you similar situations where you may receive "service with a smile" rather than grumpy employees.

Using pivoting techniques will build a strong foundation for support of all the chakras.

The sixth chakra, in the center of the forehead, is often called the third eye because, when opened and balanced, our intuition is most clear. We gain an inner sight with which we can see, so to speak, beyond the appearances. It is no coincidence that what has come to be known as the sixth sense (a highly attuned intuition) is governed by the sixth chakra.

Someone with a sixth sense can literally see things like auras, energy forms and beings in other dimensions. Those who have this gift are often great healers. However, this ability is not always a gift from the divine and does not always lend itself to great healing work.

Our culture seems to have a proclivity for glorifying psychic abilities. Yet, sometimes these abilities can indicate an imbalance in a chakra or worse; it may indicate leakage from the astral realms. The astral realm is not a place from which the wise will siphon information, but where human discordant energy—our discord—comes together forming dark entities. This energy has taken on the consciousness of its source and has the power to work against us as a negative entity or force.

There is a belief system suggesting there is no such thing as an evil or a dark force in any form. I think it is a mistake to live within the framework of such a concept. In fact, I think it very possible this belief is a control mechanism of the same force that is not supposed to exist. Negativity loves to hide, and what better disguise than nonexistence?

The astral realm is full of these "nonexistent" entities and, although there is a grain of truth in all things (usually just enough to confuse us), information from that place has little to do with God and Goddess.

Discrimination is a trait of a sub-chakra located very close to the third eye. In the Eastern Indian culture it is called the Humsa. Discrimination is vital. Take a moment or two daily to ask for discrimination or divine directing intelligence in all things. This can be very effective in protecting oneself from misguidance. It will also help one to recognize the truth and recognize people who, with a clear, strong third eye, are truly receiving insight and information from the higher realms. What indicates our degree of consciousness is not necessarily how much phenomenon we can produce, but how we handle life.

This sixth chakra profoundly connects with the third chakra. They are both closely linked to the ego. Our likes, dislikes, judgments, perceptions, our need to control as well as our ability to surrender, all have their roots in these centers. The clearer and stronger these two chakras become, the more we are able to master the ego and its activities.

When I feel and hear myself being whiny and uncharacteristically complaining, it is often my ego voicing an imbalance in my third chakra. Sahaja Yoga taught me to take notice of the third chakra whenever a floating sense of dissatisfaction crept into my world. I recently noticed I was complaining about every conceivable thing possible (and believe me, there's lots to choose from in the jungle). Sure enough, my third chakra was a bit blocked and my sixth chakra was attempting to compensate by indulging the ego. I discovered this by moving into a state of meditation (as described in Part II, Chapter 7). With practice and focus on the chakras, it becomes easy to feel and sense the condition of a chakra. I placed my hand on my solar plexus, repeating several times, "I Am satisfied." I also moved my hand in a clockwise direction over the chakra for several minutes—the natural energetic force flowing from my hand created movement in the chakra, giving way to a clearer, more free-flowing energy. As my third chakra cleared, my sixth chakra also relaxed, quieting my ego. The sense of irritated dissatisfaction dissipated and so did the whining and complaining.

Also, being selective about what visual input you allow into the sixth chakra, such as pictures and images, is important. Excessive input, especially of a negative or violent nature, can block this chakra. Cutting back on the evening news or bloody horror movies can improve the condition of this chakra.

All of the centers, particularly the sixth chakra, can benefit greatly from a technique called Thought Field Therapy (TFT).[13] Dr. Roger J. Callahan developed and teaches this technique, which consists of finger tapping in specific sequences and locations on the body. This tapping redirects the messages traveling along the energy and nervous systems. The tapping points are actually acupressure points.

Gary Craig has developed a similar technique which is becoming quite popular known as Emotional Freedom Technique (EFT).[14] I recommend trying both TFT and EFT and deciding which works best for you—it may be a combination of the two.

There are numerous and varied recipes within the practices of TFT and EFT. A simple and effective application is to first notice when you are in a state of joy or peace or love. Then take twenty or thirty seconds to tap that feeling into the sixth chakra by lightly but firmly tapping with two or three fingers on the area between and just slightly above the eyebrows. Tap in this information as often as possible along with a verbal affirmation like, "I Am joyful," or "I Am peaceful." This procedure will anchor in the desired emotional state.

After a few days of this, you can then use the technique when feeling angry, stressed or sad. Tap the sixth chakra for several seconds while breathing deeply and saying, "I release the anger (or whatever the emotion)." Then stop for a second or two and resume tapping, this time affirming "I Am joyful" or "I Am happy." This will access the previously tapped-in information and serve to release and replace the present, disturbing emotional state. This little practice can be highly effective in shedding emotional discomfort and creating energetic harmony. Thought Field Therapy is an easy and excellent technology for managing your overall energy as well as strengthening the sixth chakra.

The Seventh Chakra and Above

It is here in the magical space above us where we most clearly feel our connection to spirit. Meditating on the heart chakra provides depth, while doing so on the seventh chakra, and those above, brings us to the heights.

When this center is developed, opened and balanced, we experience greater harmony within the entire chakra system. A closed or clogged crown chakra can cause a heavy or dark feeling, like a cloud hanging over one's head. Doubt or disbelief in God can close this chakra. Resting the attention on the top of the head and above with love and the intention to communicate with the divine can develop the seventh, eighth and ninth chakras and bring us to peace.

We reach the great silence and achieve thoughtless awareness through the seventh and higher chakras. It is here where we can "hear" the answer to questions and prayers.

If we neglect our lower chakras and open these higher ones to an extreme, we may lose contact with the realities of the physical world. We see such an imbalance in individuals who appear to be flaky, flighty, ungrounded and unable to just "get it together." Yet, the crown chakra can be a great source of bliss when we care properly for our entire chakra system.

The chakras are profound gifts to be honored and well nurtured. If we think of them as holy steps leading us to our oneness with the divine, they become more than mere energy centers; they become luminous gems guiding us on the road to mastery.

A Review of the Practices in this Chapter

Using the elements:

Water: Water can have a cleansing and purifying effect particularly on the left or feminine side of the body. Soak your feet in warm water and sea salt for ten minutes in the evening to help drain away stress and imbalances in the body. Call on the beings who govern water to cleanse and purify your body and energy field.

Fire: Fire is the powerful element that clears and fortifies the right side of the body and the chakras affecting it. Looking into fire, using fire with reverence and acknowledging the beings of this element will bless us with a dynamic energy in our physical activity. Simply lighting a candle and letting it burn while we relax can presence the power of fire.

Air: Look into the sky for a few minutes everyday and acknowledge the deities who govern the air. This will help clear the upper chakras—our heart, throat and head.

Earth: Sitting on the ground, take a few moments to still the mind, place your hands, palm down, reverently on Mother Earth, and ask Her to take all negativity from you. See and feel the bottom of your body open up and release as Mother Earth literally and lovingly vacuums out the blocks and unwanted energy She may find there.

Keeping some form of each element in your immediate environment will contribute to the overall well being of your chakra system. For instance, a small water fountain; some rocks, gems, or crystals; a flame perhaps from a candle or oil lamp, and a window looking out at the sky can help create balance.

The Sixth Chakra:

When thoughts, which are immediately followed by feelings, begin to lead in a direction contradicting your master plan, don't resist. Simply muster up the strength to focus attention on something else. Anything else will do—it doesn't have to be something lofty. Just make it something different—something that makes you feel good, and is perhaps just a notch or two higher on the vibrational scale. This will work well enough to shift your energy up again.

A variation of this pivoting technique is to rely on your sixth chakra to help you reach for a thought that feels better about the same subject. Rather than switching thoughts to something else altogether, you remain focused on the same thing, except you come up with positive thoughts, leading to other positive thoughts.

Take a moment or two daily to ask for discrimination or divine directing intelligence in all things. This can be very effective in protecting oneself from misguidance.

Use TFT and/or EFT to manage your sixth chakra thoughts and the emotions they evoke. A simple and effective application is to first notice when you are in a state of joy or peace or love. Then take twenty or thirty seconds to tap that feeling into the sixth chakra by lightly but firmly tapping with two or three fingers on the area between and just slightly above the eyebrows. Tap in this information as often as possible along with a verbal affirmation like, "I Am joyful," or "I Am peaceful." This procedure will anchor in the desired emotional state.

After a few days of this, you can then use the technique when feeling angry, stressed or sad. Tap the sixth chakra for several seconds while breathing deeply and saying, "I release the anger (or whatever the emotion)." Then stop for a second or two and resume tapping, this time affirming "I Am joyful" or "I Am happy." This will access the previously tapped-in information and serve to release and replace the present, disturbing emotional state. This little practice can be highly effective in shedding emotional discomfort and creating energetic harmony. Thought Field Therapy is an easy and excellent technology for managing your overall energy as well as strengthening the sixth chakra. For more detailed procedures go to www.emofree.com.

The Throat Chakra:

This chakra is also helpful in exposing and thus expelling negative energy. Negativity loves to hide; it gains power from secrecy, which is why secrets can make us sick. Often, just by verbally naming, disclosing or identifying a problem or issue, it will vanish. The trick is to not give into the temptation to continue talking about the problem. Giving it prolonged attention will reinstate the negativity and defeat the purpose. Simply identify it, expose it, release it and move on.

The Heart Chakra:

Within the heart lies the sacred authority to channel the light and love that is our divinity. To focus and project divine love through the heart to any person or circumstance is one of the greatest activities available to us.

Begin breathing slowly in through your nose and out through your nose while gently keeping your attention on your nostrils and the breath. After a few moments, move the attention to your heart and simply say "I love you." Loving your heart will help it to open and shine. Then with an in-breath, connect the heart through the throat center with the center in the forehead, which then connects to the chakras above the head. With an out-breath through the mouth pull the light of God above your head into your heart and out into the world or directly to whatever or whomever you wish to bless and bathe in this divine light. This exercise reminds me of a fire breathing dragon! We are breathing out the pure breath of the divine and burning up any lower energies that no longer serve the desired target.

In this way, we create a continuous flow of light from our divine presence above us, down through the upper chakras, out through the heart, and then back again to the heavens. Each time we intentionally fuel this circular flow, it grows stronger.

PART II
THE VEHICLES

Mastery means the constructively qualified energy and eternal control of all energy and all substance, whenever you move anywhere in interstellar space.

— Elohim Arcturus
The "I Am" Discourses (book 14)

A Call to Mastery

Chapter 6:
SUCCESS AND FORMULAS

There is no place where you end and God begins.
— *Paula Bronte*

I have heard many people claim all they want in their life is spiritual mastery. Yet they are unwilling to "be and do" in order to "have." The concert pianist or prima ballerina did not, at the start of their careers, make a verbal announcement about their desires and then sit back and wish it would happen. They did not neglect to put forth the effort, involvement or discipline needed to manifest their desire. In fact, they probably jumped in with both feet, being propelled by the love, excitement, and joy of their mission. It depends on how much we want something.

Drawing a parallel between spiritual mastery and mastery of any other kind, we see, for instance, professional athletes or highly accomplished musicians and artists all in a state of being deeply passionate and unshakably determined. This fierce determination can be triggered and supported by external influence. However, no one can make the commitment for them. It is an inherent, undiluted facet of the soul finding expression through the remembrance of this aspect of their true, core identity.

So, first in this formula we have single-mindedness, perseverance, dedication, and a love for the desired pursuit.

Then, the one who is seeking mastery in any arena will

follow the patterns of others who have already mastered that particular achievement. They will research, study and then emulate the practice, techniques, schedules and mental and emotional training of someone or of several individuals who have previously done it successfully.

Last, they will hang out with people who are accomplished. They will spend time with people who are powerful, positive and know what it takes. Some of these people may play the role of coach, trainer, manager, colleague or friend.

This is the basic formula for success. This is how many of those who become masters in their chosen field reach those heights of skill and accomplishment.

Following along with this parallel, those who truly desire to become spiritual masters thirst for the intimate, interlocking exchange of sacred consciousness with their own life stream. They see and love their own divinity and are joyfully dedicated to expressing that divinity through mastery.

They are not only willing to "be" devoted and to "do" practices that work for them; they are delighted and grateful for the opportunity to "have" their mastery. They discover what has worked for others and, seizing what speaks to them most clearly, incorporate those methods into each day of life.

They surround themselves with others who are seeking to achieve spiritual mastery. In fact, the most powerful companions for one who is on the road to mastery are those who have already gained that supreme authority—the ascended masters.

Inviting these beings into our worlds is a very potent ingredient in this formula. The "I Am" teachings of Saint Germain offer in-depth detail about these great ones and how we can establish close relationships with them. (See Part I, Chapter 3, The Three Levels of Mastery.)

Following this format for success will be of great value to

anyone who desires to master any pursuit in life.

The Basics

Attaining mastery and the ascension differs greatly from the traditional promise of rewards to be gained later in heaven. Historically, many institutional religions were founded on this promise of future reward in order to maintain present control.

The rewards of mastering life and gaining ascension abound in great magnitude each moment of each day. Living on the road to mastery is heaven on Earth, right here, right now. Granted, some days we may feel like there's much more Earth than there is heaven. But that's okay. Feeling and being human is part of the experience. It provides us with the contrast necessary to realize who we really are. It gives us the opportunity to flex our muscles a bit. At those times, we get to reach down deep inside and pull to the surface the inner strength that will exercise our ability to shift the quality of our thoughts and emotions and, therefore, our experiences as well.

The techniques and formulas in this section may prove to be of great assistance at times when we are passionately in need of that inner strength. In the table of contents, you'll see a modest list of what I'm calling the vehicles. These techniques, suggestions, and practices are few in number compared to what is available, from both ancient and modern teachings.

Some of these vehicles may be familiar to you. Some may even sound like old news.

But these are the basics. I am including them because, well, because they *are* the basics! Without them we can get lost or even stuck in our spiritual growth.

I was a martial arts student for a number of years and, although it was more than a decade ago, I still remember our sensei with his bamboo stick and heavy Japanese accent drilling us on the basic fundamental stances and moves over and over again. He did this even with the higher-ranking belts. If we wanted to master this art, he explained, we must have strong form and powerful basic techniques. Without these, any new skills we might acquire would be weak and not worthy of people who wish to call themselves a master.

In my RET practice, I would often urge a client to spend the next week simply creating a state of gratitude, taking ten minutes a day for silent meditation or even just getting some exercise. Invariably, their reaction would be something like, "Oh yeah! I used to do that all the time! I forgot about that!" They would usually return for their next appointment eager to tell me about the success stemming from their return to the simple basics.

Many of the recently revealed techniques for attaining enlightenment are truly magnificent. Yet without a solid foundation holding us firmly engrained in our connection with the divine, these powerful tools can be reduced to mere magic tricks. The power in all things is the divine and our relationship with it.

Formulas

We seem to love formulas, the how-to methods lining it up for us in easy steps. The power in formulas is clarity. Clarity provides confidence and allows for integration; it removes our excuses for stagnation. Confusion and murkiness are excellent environments for promoting inertia. Inertia is an agent of creation by default, which feeds the perception of victim-hood and disempowerment. Deliberate creation is the intentional manifestation of our conscious will. Clarity is an important step to deliberate creation and therefore to mastery as well. For the sake of clarity, wherever possible I will present our vehicles as formulas.

Chapter 7:
FORMULA #1 – MASTERY

The spirit manifests itself to a warrior at every turn. However, this is not the entire truth. The entire truth is that the spirit reveals itself to everyone with the same intensity and consistency, but only warriors are consistently attuned to such revelations.

— Carlos Castaneda
The Wheel of Time

The primary formula underlying the achievements leading to mastery is:
- Train your Attention
- Pray, Demand, Command
- The Power of a Clear and Pure Motive

Training the Attention

Even if you disregard everything else in this book, if you write off as useless all other teachings in all other books, and the only skill you truly master is the ability to keep your attention unwaveringly fixed on the divine, true spiritual mastery can be yours. Whatever your religion or spiritual practice may be, if you spend some time—morning, noon and night—with the divine, the attention will become trained to rest there even while you are fully engaged in other activities.

"Thou shalt have no other gods before me."

This was an edict given to humanity at a time when the "other gods" were easy to spot. The idols, carved of marble, stone, and metals, were on display for all to identify easily as objects of worship. The same instruction is equally as powerful now, but the "other gods" have taken cover, hiding within the infinite stimulus of our modern world.

When we give more attention to our inner divine being than we do to the outer world, we are allowing our attention to honor that ancient instruction.

I am reminded of a journal entry I once made about a moment spent with my young Amerindian neighbor in Suriname:

"What is it like to be eight years old in a world without television?

She sits beside me, this Indian princess, regally cutting out puzzle pieces from an old coloring book. She catches me as I study the color of her skin, that smile covering the width of her bronze face.

What is it like to be eight years old in a world where there are no computer games?

Chanel sits rapt in her creations. Her focus is laser-like, her attention drips with determination and she is skilled in the art of being fully present. Her brain has not been programmed by the endless remotes that fill our electronic world. She doesn't dart from one visual to another seeking ever more stimulation, thirsting for the conquest of her own psyche."

When we put our attention, coupled with strong emotion, on any person, place, condition or thing for a period of time, we become vibrationally similar to the object of our efforts. We become that to which we give our true attention. As we give our attention to the divine, we receive in return the gift of becoming divine. Saint Germain states:

"Where your thought is, there you are; for you are your consciousness. What you think and feel, you create! And what you hold your attention upon, you become! Where your thought is, there you are; for you are that consciousness that can go everywhere."[15]

In her biography, *Seabiscuit,* Laura Hillenbrand writes of Tom Smith, the trainer and "horse whisperer" who took the racehorse Seabiscuit to his renowned victories. In referring to Tom's lifelong relationship with horses, she writes, "They had been the quiet study of his life—he had grown up in a world in which horsemanship was as essential as breathing. He was always looking at his horses. He had devoted himself to them so wholeheartedly that he was incomplete without them."

When asked about why he did not use a stopwatch in his horse training Tom said: "They take your attention off the horse." Through the power of attention Tom Smith "had become like one of them."[16] He had become like the horses to which he had devoted his life and his attention.

Where is your attention? Asking yourself this question often is an effective first step in training the attention. It can help to lasso our thoughts and emotions, thereby our attention as well, and redirect them. By asking this question, we are giving ourselves the chance to notice where our attention is and the opportunity to call it back, if we so wish, and reassign it elsewhere. We increase our ability to choose what we want and let go of what we don't want by increasing our awareness of where we are directing our attention.

We increase our ability to choose to focus our attention on the divine beings as well as our bond with them each time we ask ourselves, "Where is my attention?"

Sometimes just focusing the attention on the space a few inches above the head can improve our relationship with our attention and our capacity to control it. When the attention is above our heads, it can connect us to the divine octaves and the beings who dwell therein. It is like plugging into an electrical circuit or socket, which connects us to the main source of power.

Asking ourselves several times a day, "Where is my attention?" not only trains the attention, but also helps us discover the attention.

Is it thought?

Yes.

Is it also emotion?

Yes.

But it is more than either one of these or a combination of the two. The attention is like a silver thread upon which our life force energy flows to us from God and Goddess and from us to wherever we direct it.

By asking the question, "Where is my attention?" we are training ourselves to pay attention to our attention. By repeatedly taking our attention away from wherever it is (like annoyance or impatience at standing in a long, slow-moving line at the grocery store) and placing it a few inches above the head, we are creating a visceral experience of what attention is; we are becoming familiar with its presence. We can feel the energy and vibration of the activity we call attention as it sits in this very strategic location above our heads. (See Part I, Chapter 5: The Chakra System.)

Training the attention to sit above the head can itself be a form of meditation. This begins with sitting in a quiet, peaceful place and taking a few minutes to still the mind and relax the body. Then with your mind's eye, find a place a few inches above your head. Gently settle your attention there while breathing slowly and rhythmically. At first, you may find it helpful to picture a flame in that space or a column of light pouring down from the heavens. You may use some other symbol, but make sure the picture is a simple, singular object. The idea is to disengage the thinking mind, to enter into silence.

You may find you are able to hold your attention steady for just a few moments. As thoughts jump in and attempt to steal your attention away, simply dismiss them and return to the flame above your head. You may want to direct an angel or divine being to bring you into the silence and help keep you there. You will be able to hold it for longer periods as your attention quickly gains strength.

This meditation takes some practice, but becoming thoughtless is worth the time and effort. In fact, if done daily, it soon becomes effortless, and not only will your attention gain power, but your intuition will as well. This state of meditation also relieves stress, enhances overall well-being and leads to a masterful way of being in the world.

Further, this exercise is threefold in its benefits. It brings us into a deep state of meditation, allows for the strengthening of our attention—just as lifting weights strengthens a muscle—and allows us to understand how it feels to intentionally direct and focus our attention.

At any time of day, while sitting at a stoplight, in a business meeting, or the dentist's waiting room, we can ask ourselves, "Where is my attention?" as a reminder to direct our attention to the top of the head. As the attention becomes stronger, we no longer need to be in meditation to control it. When we find ourselves feeling upset or angry or stressed, it's a good time to ask the question—you can be sure the attention is anywhere but on the top of your head. Redirecting it there will bring your emotions more into balance. Redirecting the attention not only to the top of the head, but to other locations as well, like the heart, will help to draw you up and away from distress or frivolity.

Training the attention is so vital to achieving mastery

because if left to dwell within the darkness of unbridled negative thoughts and emotions, we will become that darkness and mastery will elude us. When our attention is on the world and the human condition thereof, we are becoming more human. When our attention is trained to easily and lovingly dwell on the divine, we become more divine.

Pray, Demand, Command

Spiritual mastery is rooted in the art of communicating with the divine. I use the word "art" not because it requires special skills, but because when it is done with love, it creates immense beauty in your life and in the world.

Mother Teresa said: "I always begin my prayer in silence. It is in the silence of the heart that God speaks. We need to listen because it's not what we say but what He says to and through us that matters. As blood is to the body, prayer is to the soul."[17]

Prayer is when we talk to God and meditation is when we listen. Of course, there are many forms of prayer and meditation. Each prayer creates a ripple of vibrational activity in accordance with the individual's personal vibration and the particular form of prayer being used.

Masters do not plead.

Masters command.

Pleading is not praying. Pleading is putting strong attention on what we don't have and on what we don't want. It emanates lack, vibrates lack, and creates a frequency and field of energy that forces the law of attraction to bring us more of what we do not want.

Commanding and decreeing is essential to manifesting and mastery because of the feeling it generates. The universe and its laws do not literally hear our words and speak our language. Rather, it connects with the current of energy and the emotion flowing from us when we put forth our prayers. When we decree, command, and demand, we are more likely to feel masterful, abundant, worthy, powerful, and in control. The universal law accepts such vibration and returns to us that which is a vibrational match.

When we pray in the form of pleading, or we affirm with a sense of lack, or we want with desperation, the universe also reads those feelings and returns to us more of the same. We cannot fool the law. We can't say one thing and feel another and expect what we say to be honored. It is our *true feelings* that will be recognized and honored. The universe reads our feelings, our vibrations, our emotions and our currents of nonphysical energy.

Let's think for a moment in terms of patterns. Imagine the universe is made of infinite patterns of energy. Imagine our thoughts, emotions and intentions are also energetic patterns. (Remember there is no duality here. We are not separate from the universe and its laws. Therefore every pattern we offer is already a part of the universe and every pattern in the universe is available to us.) When we offer the universe an intention, the energetic pattern of that intention will seek out, unite and merge with a matching universal pattern, giving us more of, or something similar to, what we started out with. This process occurs as a result of the law of attraction.

Understanding this law is the key to living a harmonious and masterful life. In order to be master of our worlds, we must first be master of ourselves. Our thoughts, feelings and intentions are the primary subjects of our mastery and the primary focus of our commands.

Asking, in fact, commanding the divine to direct our energy will line up our vibrations in such a way that we become receptive and expectant.

When we command, we align ourselves with the divine; we remind ourselves, on some level, we are truly one with the divine—not less than, in any way. However, it is vitally important to remain humble. We are by no means commanding God and Goddess to do our bidding. Rather we are commanding our own life force energy to merge with the greater energy of the divine.

Commanding, demanding and decreeing is like using a laser postal service. If given with a feeling of authority, the command puts forth a light ray upon which the heavens send back to us that for which we call.

This form of prayer has a magnetic pull, drawing to us that for which we decree and which reflects the feelings we hold while making that decree.

There is an essential order of emphasis to be applied when making a decree, command or prayer of any form. The primary function of these forms of communication is to offer ourselves as participants in the divine plan by genuinely accepting and acknowledging our authority. Regardless of what we are praying for, the first layer of intention is to convey the heartfelt message of joining the party—we claim our place as members of the divine scheme of things. It's as if we are saying, "Yes, I'm here with you, ready and willing to take my responsible position in the divine order of the universe and my own world."

Think in terms of any earthly relationship. When we are with someone who feels and sees himself or herself as less than us, lower in status or ability or esteem, we then experience a relationship imbalance, usually forcing us to take most of the responsibility and authority in that relationship and in whatever accomplishment may take place within it, thereby limiting the possibilities. On the other hand, when we are in a true partnership, there arises a mutual respect and comfort, allowing for the emergence of a third party—an unseen, but often strongly felt, energetic power lending itself to unlimited creation.

When we master this authentic alignment with God and Goddess, our presence, the ascended masters and the angels, we move into a partnership of great joy and power. We can almost hear those divine beings celebrating our arrival. It is truly as if we have arrived as the honored guest at a party given for the expansion of life.

From this place of partnership we then give the secondary, but important, emphasis on the thing, circumstance, or condition being called forth.

Jesus taught us all else would be granted to us if we put the kingdom first. Take your rightful place in the kingdom first, then clearly call for your pure desire. Remember to see your calls already fulfilled and hold a space of expectancy. The possibilities are as limitless as you allow.

At first, learning to command and demand from the divine may feel a bit uncomfortable, a little arrogant and even blasphemous for some. However, when we take a moment to first contact the deep love and adoration we feel for the divine, we can then communicate from our hearts.

Bear in mind, Jesus didn't plead or beg when healing the sick and crippled. He commanded, fully confident His Father would hear His call and fulfill it. He wholly expected His words and the powerful, intentional energy they held would manifest His will.

He knew His will and His Father's will were one.

Commanding is one of the major elements transforming a statement from a mere affirmation to an actual decree. Affirmations can raise vibrations and effectively program our deeper minds. But decrees literally call forth power from higher octaves. The potent vibration and energy generated and released through a decree spoken out loud with the full power of intention immediately sets the law of attraction into operation. We align ourselves with the ascended ones and that upon which we put our attention is drawn to us.

This form of prayer triggers the innate understanding of our divinity and mastery. Just as we direct our physical selves to act, we are privileged, in fact expected, to also direct our non-physical selves—our God-selves.

Part of the power in using this form of prayer comes from the momentum it allows us to gather. This momentum is the accumulation of energy charged with the powers of our decrees. Over time, the master builds such a strong momentum just one command or even the thought of a command can bring forth manifestation.

Building and maintaining momentum is important for those on the road to mastery. That is why it isn't recommended one start and stop several times while on this road or jump from one practice to another. These things hinder the creation of a strong momentum.

Remember, the answer is always ask—ask and keep asking.

Ask with love, authority and expectation in your mind and heart. Ask with words claiming your mastery.

Ask with clear vision and imagery and keep on asking as a powerful momentum gathers.

Ask, command, demand, call forth with pure motivation and the heavens will hear your call and honor it with love.

Clear and Pure Motive

Why do I want my mastery? It's an important question. Sometimes what is true and what we would like to believe is true are two different things. Honest reflection on this question may reveal several layers of your soul's longing. It may also instigate the ego's insatiable desire to keep you identified with its demands. What constitutes our core purpose in seeking the attention of the divine?

Wanting wealth or health or seeking solutions to our problems usually motivates us to first turn to Goddess and God. We seek divine correction for our human mistakes. Many of us receive it: "Ask and ye shall receive."

In the movement toward mastery, we find our motivation begins to shift as our intention embodies the power that springs from love and devotion. We no longer seek solutions to our problems, for with mastery comes the dissipation of our problems. As masters, we control our life and create with purpose. Creating with a clear, pure motive is a fundamental element in this formula. When we are clear about who we are as divine beings and we are pure in our desires, we are free of those obstacles that can push us off the path to mastery.

I have seen people who, because of deep, painful, unresolved insecurity, use spirituality as a means for drawing attention to themselves. They seek recognition and market themselves claiming to be "powerful," in the attempt to hide the smallness they feel inside. The danger here is that in their need for approval, these unfortunate individuals forget unto themselves they can do nothing.

Mastery is the power that comes to us and through us from Goddess/God and the light rays of the Ascended Ones. That power comes when we give our love to the divine. To seek personal recognition, separate and apart from our Source, is not an act of mastery, but enslavement by the ego.

When thinking deeply on the question, "Why do I want my mastery?" check in with your emotional self. If we call forth mastery, we must love it or it will not come. What does it mean to love mastery? I suspect for each person it feels a little different. Loving our mastery can mean loving the closeness it brings—closeness to Goddess/God, the angels, the deities, all of the divine beings. We may be motivated by the chance to have such loving friends and to spend time with them through our attention. The master calls from a space of certainty and security because clarity and purity of love guarantees fulfillment of our calls.

When we send our love and adoration to the divine, we receive it back a thousand fold. And that for which we ask is drawn to us as the love we share with the divine clothes us in a magnetic power.

Motivation is the key to fulfillment of our decrees. One of the primary emotions behind manifestation is desire. If we call for something because we think we should have it, but we don't deeply and truly want it, our decree won't carry much strength.

Remember, the universe reads our hearts.

If we call, for instance, for more time, money or health because we are truly motivated by the desire to worship and serve God and Goddess, to put our attention on the divine and cultivate that relationship free of the stresses the lack of those things can create, then our motivation and intention carry strength, clarity and purity.

Intention and motivation are closely akin to one another. In fact, the thesaurus I use lists synonyms like "aim," "goal," "purpose" and "design" to describe both of these words.

The words of a thesaurus or of any other book, including this one, cannot fully capture or convey the deep and profoundly intense mission of the soul to breathe divine life into the outer world. Such a powerful intention can bring about unexpected occurrences, orchestrate unseen activities and attract synchronistic events for the fulfillment of its cause. A truly powerful intention can have a wide-reaching and long-standing effect.

The Declaration of Independence and the Constitution of the United States of America are both, in the literal sense, just paper and ink—nothing more.

What makes them so much more is the intention and motivation held by the authors of those documents and the

power inextricably imbedded in the very signatures themselves. These men were not alone. When we stand in firm
determination and love for a purpose which expresses the
divine plan, we become more than we are. Our abilities and
energetic influence grow exponentially as the divine stands
with us, flooding forth its omnipotence.

A Review of the Practices in this Chapter

Training the Attention:
   Ask yourself several times a day: "Where is my attention?" Focus the attention on the space a few inches above
the head. When the attention is above our heads, it can connect us to the divine octaves and the beings who dwell therein. When you are in stressful situations asking the question
"where is my attention?" can redirect your attention to the
top of your head and bring your emotions more into balance.
Redirecting the attention not only to the top of the head, but
to other locations as well, like the heart, will help to draw
you up and away from distress or frivolity.
   Training the attention to sit above the head can itself be
a form of meditation. This begins with sitting in a quiet,
peaceful place and taking a few minutes to still the mind and
relax the body. Then with your mind's eye, find a place a few
inches above your head. Gently settle your attention there
while breathing slowly and rhythmically. At first, you may
find it helpful to picture a flame in that space or a column
of light pouring down from the heavens. You may use some
other symbol, but make sure the picture is a simple, singular
object. The idea is to disengage the thinking mind, to enter
into silence.
   You may find you are able to hold your attention steady

for just a few moments. As thoughts jump in and attempt to steal your attention away, simply dismiss them and return to the flame above your head. You may want to direct an angel or divine being to bring you into the silence and help keep you there. You will be able to hold it for longer periods as your attention quickly gains strength.

This state of meditation relieves stress, enhances over-all well-being and leads to a masterful way of being in the world.

Pray, Demand, Command:

Connect with the divine and speak your request—your decree, command or prayer—from your heart with strength. Here are a few examples:

- "I Am the presence of light blessing everyone in this room."
- "I call on the angels that guide and guard my life to or-chestrate (you fill in the blank)."
- "In the name of (name anyone specifically that you would like to call on—for instance, "Beloved Jesus"), I de-mand I be freed from this anger and confusion (or replace with any emotion or circumstance). I now claim perfect peace and clarity."
- "Beloved Archangel Michael and your Legions of Light, I call forth your protection and guidance for all the younger generation." Or you can direct this to all incoming souls or to someone specific like a child using drugs or anyone living in the lower energies.
- "I Am divine abundance flowing through every aspect of my life."
- "I Am the presence of God in every thought, word and deed."

The teachings of Saint Germain offer very powerful de-crees that call forth the assistance and power of specific cosmic beings and ascended masters.

The most important aspect of this practice is to understand that a decree is a statement of strong intent, with no begging or pleading involved, and is often directed to a specific divine being. State your decrees out loud with love, authority and expectation in your mind and heart.

Remember to send love to the divine. We are often so busy asking for help that we forget to just be in love with God and Goddess. When we send our love and adoration to the divine, we receive it back a thousand fold.

Clear and Pure Motive:

Ask yourself, "why do I want my spiritual mastery?" Take time to ponder this question and perhaps make a list of answers that come to you. Notice which reasons are pure desires and which are self-serving. This is not as a means of judgment, but rather as a way of deciphering which aspects of your motivation are best served by your loving attention.

Chapter 8:
FORMULA #2 – MANIFESTATION

Thoughts can never become things until they are clothed with feeling.

> — *Saint Germain*
> *Unveiled Mysteries*

No respectable book on mastery would be complete without some how-to instructions about creating and manifesting. After all, what are we becoming masters of? Of ourselves, yes. However, mastering ourselves means we are then masters of this world—masters over energy and substance.

Manifestation is an integral aspect of mastery.

Through this skill, we gain the intimate understanding that the majority of work needed to accomplish something in the outer world is actually done in the inner world. The master's creations are alive and growing in the unseen realms long (or perhaps not so long) before they appear in the physical world.

Sometimes when practicing the art of manifestation we must first be clear about what we do not want before we can gain absolute clarity about what we do want. When we create something we do not want, we have simply "missed the mark." As stated earlier, missing the mark is synonymous with sin. So, from this premise, committing a sin simply means we have been focusing on the wrong target. Determining what we want and keeping our attention on it will redefine the target and open the way to manifesting.

The formula for successful, purposeful manifestation is:
• Focused Attention
• Imaging (visualization)
• Emotional Empowerment

Several years ago, I was employed as an inside sales executive by a company selling telephone sessions with a personal coach for the purpose of financial gain and personal development.

I decided to become one of the top producers. This was more of a decision than a choice. To decide is to embrace a kind of finality—death is reflected in other "-cide" words such as homicide, suicide and genocide. We prefer to choose, because then we can feel free to choose again, to recreate. But I have found in some circumstances, when I decide rather than choose, I am better served by the homicide, suicide and genocide of the doubts, fears and excuses that can threaten my progress. I experienced this when I decided to quit smoking, when I decided to unleash my potential as a top salesperson, and when I decided to become a successful RET practitioner.

Following our outline for success, I latched onto someone who was successful and respected. He was a top producer—in the top ten percent of the sales force. Our sales were all conducted entirely by phone and ranged in price from $1,200 to $3,500 and higher. I listened in on his calls and tailored my presentations to be more like his. I took note of how he managed his time and energy and adjusted my schedule accordingly. I socialized little, except for a few moments now and then with him or one of the other top ten percent of the sales force. This helped keep my field of energy fed by positive, successful suggestions and clear of the negative energy that caused struggle for many others on the sales floor.

While doing this, I added an important ingredient of my

own. I began a simple practice I have taught many others and still use myself whenever I wish to create.

This practice began with the statement, "I Am a magnet for those people (sometimes I would use a specific number) who will most benefit from this program, have the money, and will say 'yes' to me today." I would say this maybe twenty times or more a day with conviction. The effective force of this statement was not only my clear, powerful intention, but also the first and most important point of concern— "those who will most benefit from." This statement did not revolve solely around my desire for money (although it was an important aspect as I was earning close to the six-figure range). My intention was to attract those people who would truly be well served by what I had to sell.

By putting the focus on others first and service, I was able to sidestep the personal feeling of desperation and doubt that can deflate even the most eloquent decree, especially when money is concerned.

To further strengthen this command, I added a matching visualization. At least once a day, usually in the morning, I would quiet my mind, see myself and *feel* myself go out into the cosmos among the stars and planets. Like a magnetic star with far-reaching rays, I would become a searchlight canvassing for those people who would truly benefit from my program, have the money, and say "yes" today. When I sensed I had found one, I would enfold that person, who I also saw as a star or point of light, and pull them in, bringing them into my sphere of light. If I wanted four sales that day, I would search out four points of light.

The more activity all five of our senses can contribute to our imageries, the more profound the results they reap.

Seldom would a workday pass without the number of sales I made equaling the number of people I called forth in my visualization.

While on the phone, making presentations, I was wholly engaged with a laser-like focus on that person only. I listened intently without thinking about whether I would make the sale or the money. These people were not just "sales." They were people who, like those points of light, shared with me a common intention.

This experience illustrates all three parts of our formula:

1. Focused Attention: I had that while decreeing, visualizing and on the phone.

2. Imaging: I was consistent and used as much sensory and energetic input as I could.

3. Emotional Empowerment: I empowered the process with the passion and feelings of conviction about my product, compassion and love for the people I was serving, and gratification and excitement about my success.

You can use the statement and imagery for whatever you want by altering it to fit your situation. "I Am a magnet for ..." Then become a magnetic searchlight. This process was an extremely valuable tool in building my RET practice. Integrating some form of genuine service into your creation will help keep your emotional state purified and powerful.

A Review of the Practices in this Chapter

Manifestation:

Find someone who has attained the success you desire. If it is in the area of spiritual mastery then you may choose a great teacher or an ascended master or other being of light. Call on them in your prayers and listen for their answers in your meditation. Study their lives, beliefs and practices. See what worked for them and adopt what resonates with you into your daily life. If the success you are focused on is in the areas of employment or material gain, then find some-one who has achieved what you want to manifest and find a way to follow them around or establish a relationship with them, or if they have written books, read their materials or biographies.

To manifest quickly and easily use the statement "I Am a magnet for (you fill in the blank). Couple this decree with an imagery that takes you out into the heavens and finds that which you desire. Enfold it with light and draw it into your world. Use all of your senses and give thanks that it is done.

A Call to Mastery

Chapter 9:
FORMULA #3 – THE CONSCIOUS PATH

The three jewels of the Tao: compassion, moderation and humility. Balhasar said compassion leads to courage, moderation leads to generosity, and humility leads to leadership.

— *Christopher Moore*
Lamb

The conscious path to mastery reveals ways to strengthen our spiritual power. In answering the call of the higher self we often find a precious community of great beings who are available to guide us, befriend us, and simply amplify our enjoyment of life. They are also here to teach us such things as the importance of emotions, how to guard and maintain our vibrational field, and the joys of relaxing and allowing. The formula for walking a conscious path is:
- Develop a Relationship with Divine Beings
- Create Harmony
- Mindful Protection
- The Butterflies
- Relax & Enjoy

Develop a Relationship with Divine Beings

Creating and nurturing a close relationship with the beings of light and the angels is fundamental to our experience here as masters. These great beings are now acting as the hand of God/Goddess, reaching into this octave to lift us up into the golden age. We tend to think of Jesus as the only ascended being because He is the most widely known. However, thousands of other such beings are awaiting our calls and an invitation to come into our daily lives.

When we connect with God and Goddess or the divine (or whatever name you use), there is a shotgun effect. God is infinite, and the silver thread of our attention is reaching out into a vast broadness when we seek this connection. Developing an intimate relationship with a specific energy form—such as an angel—narrows, and therefore increases the power of your focus. Like the sun on a magnifying glass creating fire, your attention gains the power of a laser-like focus.

In your prayer and meditation time, begin to seek for one with whom you resonate, with whom you *feel* a closeness. (Remember to use a protective light to guard against intrusion from the lower realms.) Then make yourself available, offer them your love and attention. They choose us; we don't choose them. Yet, by calling forth to them, asking for personal instruction and expansion of our consciousness, we let them know, by free will, our desire for a close relationship. And, of course, the law of attraction kicks in and we begin to take on the consciousness of the one upon whom we put our attention.

The ascended ones and the angels can only help us if we ask them to do so. I often have the image of these great beings standing around us, with their hands behind their backs, just waiting and longing for us to ask for help. They want us to put them to work for us in our world. Free will prevents them from acting independently of our requests.

You may be familiar with some of the masters or angels like Jesus, His Mother Mary, Quan Yin, Buddha, Krishna, and the Archangel Michael. You may choose to go to one of these or you may discover someone who is new to you. (Both Sahaja Yoga and the "I Am" Activity offer much information about this subject.) These majestic rays of light are not only available to us, but are eager to assist us. Speak their names often. After all, when you wish to get the attention of another person, you call them by name. Calling a light being by name will get its attention as well. It also brings us closer to them, allowing us to absorb some of their divine consciousness into our own. Using the name of something brings us in touch with the form of that thing.

At some level of consciousness, we clearly see that the names, terms, labels and titles we use for these sacred states and beings are all referring to one limitless divine power. God has been the traditional term, but even that one—especially that one—has its multitudinous meanings and connotations. The compartmentalizing, defining and naming of the divine is a way to wrap our minds around something we otherwise could not comprehend. It allows for the unfolding of a functional, working relationship.

Perhaps this individualizing of the divine into beings, such as angels and masters, is being done for us as an act of grace, to help us grow and expand into a level of consciousness that will allow for ease in our eventual immersion with the vastness that is God and Goddess. Until we reach that level of mastery, we can gain extreme power through our relationships with these beings.

Once you establish these relationships, nurture them. If you were fostering a friendship with another person, what would you do? You would spend time with her. You would tell her how you feel about her and express your appreciation. You would give her your attention and listen closely when she speaks to you. Light beings of higher realms can and will respond to all of this. They may be the best friends you will ever have.

Create Harmony

Create the harmony required in your feeling world to allow these great beings to enter your life and be a sustaining force in the attainment of mastery.

We have (at least) four levels, or layers, of energetic activity surrounding us, like circles. Beginning with the body, we have the physical level, extending outward and around us for about one to two feet. Then we have the emotional level, the mental level, and finally the spiritual level. These spheres or circles continue to repeat this pattern as they move further and further out and around us. These layers are often referred to as our "worlds." These worlds compose the one individualized world in which each person lives, within the bigger, global world. As many human beings as we have on Earth, there are that many individual worlds. And each individual world is the sum of the vibrational frequency of these levels of energetic activity.

The feeling world is, in many ways, the dominant player in this pattern. The vibrational quality of that layer of our energetic presence determines, to a great extent, the conditions of the vibrational quality of all the other layers. When we entertain an emotion for a while that vibrates at the lower end of the frequency scale, like anger or hate, we find our health compromised (the physical world), our thoughts and self-talk taking on a negative voice (the mental world—sometimes this is where destructive energy begins and then contaminates the feeling world), and our spiritual world becomes thickly veiled.

The feeling world is the portal through which the beings of light join us and forge relationships with us, bringing joy and mastery. Their light rays can filter through to us when the feeling world is in harmony. To be harmonious means to be congruent. This means being of a vibration that matches and mixes well with the surrounding vibrations. In music, a melodic tune's vibrational waves harmonize. A discordant tune has notes and chords working against each other and resisting a harmonious flow.

When our feeling world is saturated with resistant, discordant emotion, the light rays of the great ones do not always permeate to the degree necessary to fulfill our prayers or calls, or establish that close friendship we are seeking.

If our feeling world is holding harmonious emotions, those light rays can mix and blend and pour into, not only our feeling world, but all other levels as well. Thus, we create an overall, individualized world congruent with creating and nurturing a strong relationship with the ascended masters and angels and all that is divine.

Being with, expressing and clearing our emotions are basic to our well-being. But endless wallowing in self-pity or self-hatred is not. Carolyn Myss refers to the continuous stuckness of our emotional pain and the language surrounding it as "woundology."

I have seen many people desperately hold onto their stories, perpetuating the wounds of the feeling world and speaking the woundology needed to maintain their woundedness, thus preventing themselves from healing. When we allow ourselves to heal, we abandon our smallness. Our emotional pain keeps us buried under the weight and safety of our own personal little world. How can we possibly contribute to mankind or our own mastery when all of our energy and attention is being invested in the wounds that are ensuring our smallness?

In smallness there is safety. We are safe from the risks and responsibilities associated with showing up and stepping into beingness. Freeing our feeling world of low-frequency emotions and keeping it clear can bring great joy and create an environment where smallness loses its appeal and being big is no longer frightening.

Becoming conscious about feelings of irritation, anger, hatred, criticism, blame or condemnation and governing those emotions is paramount to achieving mastery. When we slide into the quicksand of these emotions, we are actually tapping into the mass accumulation of everyone else's negative emotions, thus inviting the anger and hatred of the mass consciousness into our feeling world. We don't want to do that.

Controlling our indulgences in these emotions by shifting our attention to something else entirely—something that feels better—can help keep our feeling world clear. Meditation, prayer, Rapid Eye Technology, or other forms of release therapy can also be tremendously helpful in this regard.

I'm not suggesting we deny our feelings and emotional issues, but rather that we do not allow ourselves to be controlled by them. Our emotions can be a tool to reveal deeply hidden wounds begging to be healed. They can also act as a vital part of our inner guidance system.

Our feelings act as a barometer, indicating if we are putting our attention on what we want or on what we don't want. When we feel light, uplifted and joyful, our attention is probably on what we want. When it is dark, heavy and tense, it is likely we are focusing on what we don't want. Mastery is not about whether we have fear, anger or any other emotion; it is about what we do with those emotions and the integrity with which we express them in our daily lives.

It is also helpful to remember that our attention, and therefore our emotions, can get stuck on something negative because of our mind's resistance to it. The old saying "that which we resist, persists" is still true. Acceptance plays an important role here. Acceptance, not approval or condoning, but simple, surrendered acceptance of what is, as it is, will overstep the tendency to resist, thus giving the attention freedom to move elsewhere.

No matter how far on the road to mastery we are, we will all experience some form of irritation, hurt or anger. Call it back and disappear it in a flame, lightening bolt, explosion or whatever your power of imagery chooses. Some form of fire is preferable.

The teachings of Saint Germain share with us the gift of the "Violet Flame." This is a powerful tool and when called forth will purify that to which it is directed.

I have known people who, try as they may, have simply been unable to overcome the problems plaguing them.

Donna Eden, author of *Energy Medicine,* eloquently explains this phenomenon:

"It is easy for some people to tell others to just get beyond their pain or sorrows or wounds, and it is a great idea. But I have had many people come to me who have worked very hard and sincerely, though unsuccessfully, to resolve physical or emotional injuries from long ago. The issue for many of these people is not that they wallow in self-pity, want sympathy, long to hold on to the past, need to bond with others over their misfortunes, or lack courage. The invisible but decisive factor in many of these cases is a field of habit that is outside their awareness and thus their control. Human will and intention are powerful, but if all your energies are going in the opposite direction of your will, best focus your will on changing those energies."[18]

Authentic energy work (such as Ms. Eden teaches) and release therapies (such as RET) have, in my experience, been vital in assisting such people in "changing those energies."

Mindful Protection

Our energy fields—those physical, mental, emotional, and spiritual layers constituting our world—are permeable, and so the master is mindful about maintaining a shielding presence. We have all had the experience of picking up others' energies. Sometimes we know that's why we are feeling "off." Sometimes we don't even realize we have been "slimed." We share energy in the form of thoughts, feelings, even the molecules of our breath, all the time. To protect ourselves from taking on unwanted energy from another's feeling world or energy field in general is an act of wisdom.

That is not to say we approach this protection from fear or anxiety. We simply act from awareness. Being a detached witness is among the highest forms of protection. In this state, we are free to see, hear or be in the presence of a full range of emotional and energetic vibrations without being adversely effected by them.

Reaching this state is sometimes easier said than done. The witness is anchored within the inner body, allowing for the emergence of a detached observer. Being detached and moving in the world as a witness is a primary aspect of the practice of Sahaja Yoga and many other spiritual pursuits. It is a natural by-product of the inner peace that comes from daily meditation, a clear, strong chakra system and a well-managed emotional body.

The witness state provides us with a highly effective shield because, as a "watcher," we step back from the illusion of imperfection; we are not emotionally enrolled in the "maya" being played out before us.

In other words, as a detached witness, we are free from judgment. We are not subject to the extreme emotional reactions that can hook us into an undesirable energetic pattern or allow our vibrations to be infiltrated by unwanted energy.

Judgment is not one of those barren thoughts that can innocently and ineffectively come and go. Judgment immediately attaches to itself strong emotion. Strong emotion, even positive emotion, can affect our feeling world in such a way that we become enmeshed in outer conditions and lose our balanced harmony—an important part of mastery.

Detachment and compassion are not mutually exclusive. To the contrary, being a witness enhances our ability to be compassionate. When we are not functioning from an over-taxed feeling world, we are not so subject to the temptation of sympathy, an emotion often misrepresented as compassion.

Sympathy and compassion are very different agents. Sympathy pulls us into the drama, thus making us a part of it. Compassion is a power raising us above the drama, empowering us to pour forth healing love and light and call forth divine assistance.

What does or does not permeate our energy layers is ultimately up to us. Something cannot deeply enter our field unless we invite it in through our emotional reaction to it. Being the witness is a powerful way to manage our feeling world.

Other helpful methods in protecting and keeping our emotions pure and balanced take on a more physical and mental role. It's fun to call forth a protective light while also visualizing it around you. Move your right hand up and around with intention, forming a golden arch over your head, and sweep it down and around your body. This will encase your body in a protective garment. You may charge this garment of light to pour forth divine love to everyone and everything you contact that day. In this way, you not only form a guard for yourself but you protect and serve others as well.

The solar plexus is the point in the body through which we can most easily take in negative energy. Try seeing a white and gold light pour forth from this center of power, enfolding your entire body and energy field. It feels as if this not only adds extra protection for this chakra, but strengthens it also.

Integrate some form of protection into your daily practice. Do not fool yourself into believing you are beyond the need for such things.

In Chapter 2: Global Purification and the Next Golden Age, I referred to the vehicles and how they may assist us to move though individual energetic purification as well as global purification. Some of us are more directly affected than others, like the relatives of those who died on September 11, 2001, the soldiers and citizens in Iraq, the survivors of earthquakes, and other natural disasters—the list is extensive. The victims who pay so dearly for our creations must be held in our prayers as we ask the cosmic beings to comfort and fill them with love surpassing such pain and bring them into divine peace.

For those of us indirectly affected, the true enemy is less obvious. The utter fear and devastation of these occurrences, carries through all of our feeling worlds a vibration of great distress. The emotional and psychological result of the present turmoil on Earth is, in itself, capable of creating more and even greater devastation. If our feeling worlds become contaminated with this hate, fear and pain, we will spiral into greater darkness. This is not necessary. We have the choice; we can rise above it.

Ask to be emotionally and vibrationally unaffected by any negative activity of the outer world coming within your scope of sensory perception, except for the strengthening of your compassion.

We cannot and should not stick our heads in the sand and avoid what is all around us. However, we can be discerning about what and how much distressing information we allow to infiltrate our consciousness. When we are exposed to such information we can fearlessly ask, with authority, to be protected from its vibration while also praying for everyone concerned.

This is not so much about us and our abilities or powers

as it is about the ascended masters and all beings of light. The only power we need is the ability to clearly and consistently ask for what is needed, to be harmonious enough to receive it, and to genuinely expect it. The rest is up to them.

As we vibrate more and more at the rate of mastery, our radiation becomes a healing presence. The divine light rays will flow through us and from us and, not only will we be free of negative vibratory influence but we will be a healing force as well. And if there is something we can do on the physical level to help the situation our higher selves will give us the direction and courage needed.

Any one of the techniques in this section will assist us in being with the present state of affairs—whether in regard to the world or an individual personal purification.

Upon going to bed at night, make sure a conversation with God is the last thing your mind registers—not the news programs. Walk away from or change the subject when someone is slinging negativity around your field. Simple, common sense practices requiring only your awareness and discretion can serve to help keep your feeling world in order, thereby keeping in greater service to the light.

When you do see or hear an appearance of outer discord, don't balk or panic—such fearful reaction is an invitation, an open door. Instead, claim your mastery and call for the strength to be present and the ability to be detached. The purification process does not have to be unnerving. Rely now more than ever on your divine relationships. Remember to be grateful for the great cleansing that is freeing us all.

The Butterflies

We are best protected when we are in a state of peace and love. Often we find negativity cannot bear to come near the presence of light. Mother Nature offers us Her own lesson on this method of defense.

Here in the jungle, there are very large and beautiful butterflies. They will often sit on a leaf or a blade of grass with their wings closed. When a predator approaches, they calmly open their wings. The magnificence and beauty of their color stupefies the enemy, causing them to retreat. Indeed, the beauty that is mastery is its own best shield.

Relax & Enjoy

When we become too intense about anything—even gaining our mastery—we create a contradictory, resistant vibration that can clog the flow of our creative juices. Whether we are creating a greater closeness to the divine or manifesting a new house, it pays to relax.

Relax into it all—with confidence.

Remember to breathe.

Creating is not something to be anxious about; it is a lifelong game to be enjoyed.

When we saunter through the grocery store, we don't usually stress about whether we'll get to take home what we've chosen to put in our basket. We just take what we want and/or need and know in a short time we will have these things in our worlds for our use, consumption and enjoyment.

Yet many of us have had those mortifying moments when the total at the cash register was greater than the total in our pockets. It's not fun making everyone in line wait as they watch us go though the stressful process of choosing which items to discard and which to keep.

If you are experiencing this kind of tension in your spiritual practices, make a shift to the first scenario. Choose what you put in your basket with deliberate intention and know it is yours. Jesus had no stress or doubts when He called for something He wanted. Yet He was detached about the outcome.

The master desires wholeheartedly and is surrendered to God's will at the same time. Want what you want, fully, consciously and from a pure, clear motive. Then, be satisfied in the Now, in the presence and all it holds for you, so regardless of whether or not you get what you call for, you can be happy and at peace.

There is a great Jewish saying that, in personifying God, puts this in perspective: "We plan and God laughs."

Sometimes divine will or even our own karma has other plans for us.

"I will my will to be God's will."

The internalization of this statement can take us to the deep realization that my will and God's will can be one because we are, in fact, one.

I Am that I Am.

Until we expand into the boundless realms of oneness, our finite minds can only desire in finite ways. The magnitude of the blessings the divine mind holds for us is far greater than anything we can imagine for ourselves.

When I'm manifesting, I leave room for more—for greater—just in case the divine has more in mind for me than I do.

Be relaxed about the results of your efforts. Know the unmanifested belongs to you and it awaits your call—the call that brings it into this world—into divine expression.

A Review of the Practices in this Chapter

Develop a Relationship with Divine Beings:
In your prayer and meditation time, begin to seek for one with whom you resonate, with whom you *feel* a closeness.

(Remember to use a protective light to guard against intrusion from the lower realms.) Then make yourself available, offer them your love and attention. They choose us; we don't choose them. Yet, by calling forth to them, asking for personal instruction and expansion of our consciousness, we let them know, by free will, our desire for a close relationship. And, of course, the law of attraction kicks in and we begin to take on the consciousness of the one upon whom we put our attention.

Speak their names often. After all, when you wish to get the attention of another person, you call them by name. Calling a light being by name will get its attention as well. It also brings us closer to them, allowing us to absorb some of their divine consciousness into our own. Using the name of something brings us in touch with the form of that thing.

Once you establish these relationships, nurture them. If you were fostering a friendship with another person, what would you do? You would spend time with her. You would tell her how you feel about her and express your appreciation. You would give her your attention and listen closely to her when she speaks to you. Light beings of higher realms can and will respond to all of this. They may be the best friends you will ever have.

Create Harmony:

No matter how far on the road to mastery we are, we will all experience some form of irritation, hurt or anger. Call it back and disappear it in a flame, lightning bolt, explosion or whatever your power of imagery chooses. Some form of fire is preferable.

The teachings of Saint Germain share with us the gift of the "Violet Flame." This is a powerful tool and when called forth will purify that to which it is directed.

Mindful Protection:

Be a detached witness. Practice looking at a situation and saying "that's just energy and I am the observer." Ask your presence to bring you into compassion and free you from sympathy. In compassion we can extend light and stay detached, in sympathy we get enmeshed and loose our objectivity and our ability to serve.

Other helpful methods in protecting and keeping our emotions pure and balanced take on a more physical and mental role. It's fun to call forth a protective light while also visualizing it around you. Move your right hand up and around with intention, forming a golden arch over your head, and sweep it down and around your body. This will encase your body in a protective garment. You may charge this garment of light to pour forth divine love to everyone and everything you contact that day. In this way, you not only form a guard for yourself but you protect and serve others as well.

The solar plexus is the point in the body through which we can most easily take in negative energy. Try seeing a white and gold light pour forth from this center of power, enfolding your entire body and energy field. It feels as if this not only adds extra protection for this chakra, but also strengthens it.

Ask to be emotionally and vibrationally unaffected by any negative activity of the outer world coming within your scope of sensory perception, except for the strengthening of your compassion.

Upon going to bed at night, make sure a conversation with God is the last thing your mind registers—not the news programs. Walk away from or change the subject when someone is slinging negativity around your field. Simple, common sense practices requiring only your awareness and discretion can serve to help keep your feeling world in order, thereby keeping in greater service to the light.

When you do see or hear an appearance of outer discord, don't balk or panic—such fearful reaction is an invitation, an open door. Instead, claim your mastery and call for the strength to be present and the ability to be detached.

Relax & Enjoy

Remember to breathe! We can hold tension in our bodies and it is very skilled at helping us forget to breathe. Take time to do ten to fifteen deep, belly breaths, in through your nose and out through your mouth. Someone once told me it is impossible to be afraid and breathe at the same time. I have come to experience that as truth.

Chapter 10:
FORMULA #4 – THE SIMPLE STUFF

To become a miracle worker means to take part in a spiritual underground that's revitalizing the world, participating in a revolution of the world's values at the deepest possible level. That doesn't mean you announce this to anyone ... Miracle workers learn to keep their own counsel.

— *Marianne Williamson*
A Return to Love

The following chapter is about those simple things that can have a significant impact on the quality of our lives. These are concepts and practices that can be easily forgotten but powerfully effective – when we remember to use them. Here is a loving reminder of the simple stuff:

- Mum's the Word
- Trust
- Gratitude
- Taking Action
- Peace before Action
- Miracles

Mum's the Word

Ever watch water boil? All that substance just evaporates—disappears—dissipates. When we talk (prematurely) about creations we have cooking in the ethers, we dissipate the energy—energy required to bring those manifestations into this dimension. At first, our prayers, decrees and visualizations are building a momentum. If we talk too much with too many people about our intentions and creations, before that momentum can become self-perpetuating, we are deflating the momentum and therefore the creation as well. It is like pumping air into a tire with a sizable hole in it; we are pouring forth our creative powers only to evaporate them through indiscriminate talk. (The master hasn't much need to brag or even to confide in others; conversing with the divine, the Source of his or her creation, is often enough.)

Once you feel quietly assured your momentum has gathered enough strength to bring your creation forward then you may consider confiding in someone you trust.

Who you choose to tell about your manifestations is important. Someone who might have any negative thoughts or feelings of doubt or criticism, even if unspoken, can potentially thwart your efforts. During the inception of your creations you will want to keep the energy as pure and free from outside judgment as possible.

Remember to write it down. Putting it on paper will not only help to satisfy your longing to tell somebody, but scripting holds within itself a mighty power. When we write our plans, hopes, dreams and intentions it brings a magical life to them, as if the ink itself animates them and sets them free.

An eternal record of intention is registered within the etheric plane when we express our hearts through the written word. That record has inherent potential to manifest on this plane when, through our harmonious attention, we allow it to do so.

Trust

Almost all of what is being said in this book requires

trust—trust in ourselves and in the divine. Many of my RET clients deeply struggled when it came to trusting God. Horrific traumas, abuses and betrayal often experienced in childhood, coupled with religious belief systems, left these people to relate to God and themselves in fragmented and dysfunctional ways.

When children are abandoned and betrayed by their parents or other "honored" adults they become distrustful of God. When we are children, we regard our parents as God; they are one and the same in the eyes of the victim.

This early imprint of betrayal often leaves a cellular fear and distrust permeating all relationships, including the first and most important one—the relationship with the Self.

When we grow up with the perception of victim, we project—and thereby create—circumstances supporting and proving that perception.

We find these people choosing partners who will abuse or betray them in some way. They sabotage career opportunities, rob themselves of intimate friendships and pray, believing their prayers will not be answered.

This programming of how we see the world and ourselves also makes our view of the divine terribly distorted.

In my practice, these clients and I first work together to release the imprints of abuse and betrayal through the RET techniques and the assignments they do between sessions. Once these issues begin to clear from the neuropathways, we then work on restoring (or sometimes creating for the first time) a healthy, loving, trusting relationship with God and Goddess. Learning to trust is a delicate part of our journey that requires great courage.

With the self-image of undeserving victim lifted, the image of God as an unforgiving, merciless judge also begins to lift. For those many whose hearts and minds are buried under the lies of the orthodox religions they follow, my approach is to help them discover a new God, a different God, one that had nothing to do with the guilt, shame and anger of their past.

I encourage them to read and study and experience different spiritual teachings until they find one that can feed their soul and invite the process of trust to take root.

Seeking and discovering the divine in unfamiliar territory can be a precious means for self-intimacy and freedom; it can redefine our way of being in the world.

It always comes down to attention. Shifting the attention from what was and what is, to what could be and what is wanted can take us from pain to peace, from fear to trust.

Donna Eden writes: "Energy flows where attention goes. But the opposite is also true: attention goes where energy flows. To change your mind, change your energy. You can't will happiness. You can't always will pain to stop. You cannot even will inspiration. But you can shift your energies in ways that support your happiness, diminish your pain, and increase your inspiration."[19]

I encourage anyone who struggles with this issue of trust in God to find a different God. Force your attention and your energy to take a big leap—a leap of faith to a place where a new God resides—one you can trust—a God and Goddess that will help you answer the call to mastery.

Gratitude

The cellular response resulting from the feelings of genuine appreciation and gratitude is extremely healing, uplifting and cleansing. Gratitude moves our vibrations into a very high place. Pray it, see it, feel it, breathe it, and soon you will find the entire world has changed.

When we are struggling with problems and seem unable to generate this powerful feeling, that's the time to "count your blessings." Find something—anything—that triggers gratitude. Whatever you can appreciate, no matter how small, will act as a bridge to higher ground. In the Abraham-Hicks teachings,[20] Abraham tells us that when we vibrate gratitude we literally swing the doors open, allowing divine substance to flow forth and take form as physical manifestations.

If a heavy heart is causing gratitude to elude you, then imagine for just a moment life without something dear to you. For instance, life without your hands or feet, your eyes, your spouse or children, your car, running hot water and indoor plumbing, and so on. Get the idea? Once you are breathing, eating and sleeping appreciation and gratitude, your vibrations will be much more attractive to other vibrations of a higher frequency. In reference to the law of attraction, affinity does not tolerate distance.

Through gratitude, you will have opened the portal to the unseen universal substance, thus thinning, or perhaps shedding altogether, the veil between the physical octave and the experience of limitlessness. From that vibration, it becomes much easier to put your attention on what you desire rather than on what you don't have.

Also, remember you can always just ask. Ask the divine to fill you with gratitude and help you find something to deeply appreciate. Listen and look for the answers. They may come sometimes in unexpected ways. Intend everyday to look only for what makes you feel good and brings a sense of love and appreciation into your feeling world.

Taking Action

Spirituality is not a spectator sport. It is something we live and is lived through us. We can no longer afford (we never really could) to fill coffee houses and cocktail parties with passive intellectualizing, theorizing, and philosophizing about God.

This is a time in our history when we must actively pursue our divinity. The road leading to mastery is one of meditation, contemplation and enlightening revelations, yes, but it is also one of action. We must *be* spiritual beings, and *do* spiritual actions engaging the spirit, in order to *have* mastery. Mastery is the harmonious union of *being* and *doing,* creating the *having* intended by us or the divine or both.

In her book *Life's Companion: Journal Writing as a Spiritual Quest,* Christina Baldwin shares with us this insight:

"There are really only two things to do: one is be still and listen, the other is to take spiritually based action. Everything else is bogus activity which only gets in the way of our real understanding."[21]

For each person, in any given situation, the required action differs. Consistently ask to be led to right action and you will be—if you are listening. It may be community work or political in nature; it may mean learning one of the healing arts, redefining your role in the workplace, or becoming more vocal about such things as human rights within that environment. It may just be a simple act of kindness, a moment when you step outside yourself acting for another's welfare because somewhere within you understand there is only one of us. Spiritual action definitely includes daily prayer, not empty rote and repetition, but intimate conscious communion with whatever you consider to be the divine, experienced from the heart.

Know whatever action you take will be powered by the strength and clarity of your intention. The time of holy men sitting in their caves waiting for enlightenment is over. Mastery now calls us into the world as active participants in a divine plan.

The choices we sometimes make when we have time alone, for ourselves, can either breathe life into our spiritual journey or keep us stagnant at our present level of consciousness:

Turn on the TV, or sit in meditation and turn off the thoughts.

Pick up the phone and casually call a friend, or light a candle and call on Goddess and God.

Eat an extra piece of cake to take our minds off whatever is tormenting us, or write an extra journal page addressed to an angel asking for freedom from those torments.

Such seemingly small choices, the ones we make when no one is around and we have only ourselves to contend with, are the choices that can "prime the pump" for our action in the world as spiritual masters.

Peace Before Action

"Peace before action."

This phrase recently came to me in a dream. As I awoke, the obvious drift of this statement was clear, but I sensed there was a deeper meaning and it was meant to find its way into this book. So I asked to understand the insight intended for me in the words: peace before action.

During the following few days, I remembered the phrase my mother often tried to etch into my brain: "Think before you act." This was intended to help a rash teenager exert some semblance of self-control before wreaking havoc on herself and everyone around her.

If we think before we act, we can often prevent ourselves from doing or saying something we will later regret. "Peace before action" far expands this concept into the realms of mastery. If our feeling world can actually be in an authentic vibratory state of peace when executing any activity in the physical world, that peace will infiltrate not only that particular action, but will ripple through the physical realm for some distance. The more profound the level of peace, the further the ripple effect will flow.

As masters and masters in the making, we are privileged to serve the world in such ways. The dream did not say, "love before action" or "joy" or "compassion" or any of the many other powerful states of being available to us. It said peace. I believe this to be of great significance at a time when humanity finds itself in such an "un-peaceful" state.

Regardless of where we are on the road to mastery, if enough of us begin today to genuinely practice the art of stepping into a space of peace before we do anything in the outer world, we will make a powerful impact upon each other and be of great service to the light.

It doesn't matter how fragile our state of peace may be; just begin and it will grow stronger everyday. The angels and great beings will recognize our effort and intention and assist us into greater and greater "peace before action." It also matters not how small the action. If your intention is clear, any activity in the physical realm can serve as a vehicle for your peace to spread. In this way, we can choose to charge all physical action with the powers and peace of the heavens.

Miracles

Masters perform miracles. This is a widely held misconception. Miracles are not "performable," nor are they subject to magnitude. Miracles are the unfolding of divine intention, unobstructed by human interference.

If we think for a moment in terms of waves or rays, we can imagine moving forward within the boundaries of these. If we see a wall or obstacle of some kind intruded upon the wave or ray, it is easy to imagine any movement would be deflected or redirected—being forced to step, for the time being, outside the boundaries of the wave or ray. While we are within the perimeters of that ray or wave, we are surrounded by and have access to universal substance. Universal substance is the pure limitless energy from which we as creators create. We infuse pure energy with our attention, thoughts, intentions and emotions, thus molding it to become what we desire, either deliberately or by default.

When we are forced outside of the ray or wave by obstructions of fear, greed, doubt or anything that is not love (the word love as used in this book is not in reference to the emotion of love, but rather to the power of love which heals and perfects all things), we lose access to that universal substance in its pure form. The substance from which we are then creating is that same universal substance, however it is no longer pure. It has been requalified by thoughts and emotions, which vibrate at a low, heavy rate, creating an atmosphere of density.

Miracles are the result of movement within a light ray which is free of any interference that would remove us from that ray. In other words, miracles are the natural occurrence of a sustained, harmonious life gathering the momentum necessary to out-picture the universal substance as it is divinely given to us in its pure form, qualified only by love.

So miracles are not something we do or perform; they are a state of being.

They spring from our acknowledgment, acceptance and expression of our dominion over all things and conditions in this world. They are not measurable by magnitude because they all reflect the same energy—the pure universal substance—which is infinite and beyond any form of measurement.

It requires the same degree of mastery to instantaneously heal a cold as it does to precipitate a pile of gold. However, somewhere between the cold and the gold we usually throw an obstacle like doubt into the ray, thus removing us from that vibration and preventing ourselves from being in a state of vibration that would allow the universal substance to be molded according to the higher desire.

Jesus is known for His miracles. When He saw human suffering, He did not allow it to take Him out of His vibrational wave. Instead, remaining in such a high frequency of energy, He saw only perfection. He qualified pure substance with the power of love, manifesting the perfection He saw and gathered through the momentum He had built in the light ray known as the Christ energy.

Using another analogy, remember back to when you were in school. If your pen ran out of ink or you lost your pencil, you were integrated enough in your environment that you would readily ask for one, either from the teacher or someone sitting around you. A pen or pencil is a small thing and not too much to ask for. You fully expected someone would give you a replacement. In fact, you probably even had a subtle sense it was your right to get one, as you were there and ready to work. You didn't have much emotion around the event except the desire for a writing utensil. You would almost always get one and just go on with your work.

That scenario has all the elements of effortless creation: harmony, asking, expecting, desiring, freedom from much negative emotion and the judgment you're not asking for too much. You created the replacement. Now, by mastering our attention, we can be just as comfortable and harmonious in the higher vibratory states as you were in class. In these states, the teachers and those around you are the masters, angels and light beings. If we need or want something, we just ask for it and expect it. However, here anything and everything we ask for, no matter how big or small, is subject to the same qualifiers as the pen or pencil—it's not too much to ask for nor is it too insignificant and it is our right to get it.

The only difference between that experience in school

and the experience of miracles is the maintenance of a high vibratory state and remembering that nothing is too big or too small, for everything comes from pure universal substance and it is your right to call it forth into your world.

Miracles and Service

There are so many worthwhile ways to be of service in our world. Charities, volunteer work, hospices—the avenues for helping our fellow human beings are endless. However, the ultimate service to humanity is the achievement of our own mastery. It may sound too selfish and not of service at all to think of gaining something for ourselves—even our mastery. Nevertheless, in mastery, the power of our radiation acts as the catalyst for such enormous transformation in the world that, if enough of us were capable of radiating that energy, other types of service would no longer be needed.

Jesus simply showed up and miracles followed. People were healed in ways no action-oriented service could have done. The dead were awakened and souls were purified because, in His presence, the atmosphere became charged with His Father's love.

The miracles Christ revealed to us were just a glimpse into the kingdom of which He so often spoke. His miracles and vibratory radiation were shared with us as an example of the greatest form of service to humanity.

A Review of the Practices in this Chapter

Mum's the Word:

Write your plans, goals, dreams and desires on paper. Do this in the form of a list or perhaps a letter to a divine being or your own presence. Keep quiet about these things until they have shown up in the physical realm. If you choose to share them with someone before they are fully manifested make sure it is someone who will help hold the light for you and not shed any doubts or fear.

Gratitude:

Imagine for just a moment life without something dear to you. For instance, life without your hands or feet, your eyes, your spouse or children, your car, running hot water and indoor plumbing, and so on. Can you feel an instant renewed appreciation for these things? Once you are breathing, eating and sleeping appreciation and gratitude, your vibrations will be much more attractive to other vibrations of a higher frequency. In reference to the law of attraction, affinity does not tolerate distance.

Also, remember you can always just ask. Ask the divine to fill you with gratitude and help you find something to deeply appreciate. Listen and look for the answers. They may come sometimes in unexpected ways. Intend everyday to look only for what makes you feel good and brings a sense of love and appreciation into your feeling world.

Taking Action:

Consistently ask to be led to right action and you will be—if you are listening. It may be community work or political in nature; it may mean learning one of the healing arts, redefining your role in the workplace or becoming more vocal about such things as human rights within that environment. It may just be a simple act of kindness, a moment when you step outside yourself acting for another's welfare because somewhere within, you understand there is only one of us. Spiritual action definitely includes daily prayer, not empty rote and repetition, but intimate conscious communion with whatever you consider to be the divine, experienced from the heart.

Peace Before Action:

Call forth a feeling that is an authentic vibratory state of peace before executing any activity in the physical world. That peace will infiltrate not only that particular action, but will ripple through the physical realm for some distance. The more profound the level of peace, the further the ripple effect will flow.

Regardless of where you are on the road to mastery, begin today to genuinely practice the art of stepping into a space of peace before doing anything in the outer world.

It doesn't matter how fragile your state of peace may be; just begin and it will grow stronger everyday.

PART III
TRAVEL LIGHT

You always hold the power and control of your own life experience. The only reason that you could ever experience something other than what you desire is because you are giving the majority of your attention to something other than what you desire.

— Esther and Jerry Hicks
Ask and It Is Given

Chapter 11:
THE BODY TEMPLE

Don't you wanna be where there's strength and love in the place of fear?

— Jackson Browne

The road to mastery can be arduous and tiresome if we lug our baggage along with us. We can find ourselves trudging along slowly, unable to enjoy the journey, wanting only to arrive at our destiny so we may lay down our burdens. The road to mastery is one of light leading only to more light. In order to experience the joys of this road, we must truly travel light—on all levels.

On the physical level, we are faced with many choices. "You are what you eat" is one of those clichés wise to honor. When I first began to realize that many people who are on a spiritual path are very discriminating about what substances they put into their bodies, I was skeptical. My questions were something like, "What's more powerful, me or that steak?" (I believed I was light-years ahead of any dead cow.) "Does that bottle of beer have the power to keep me from God?" (Naw. If anything, all that nutrition must be food for the soul.) However, over time I gained a deeper understanding and respect for my body as a temple—The Temple of the Most High Living God and Goddess.

If we were to take a clear, empty glass pipe and pour water through it, water would flow swiftly and easily. If we were to insert substances that clog or corrode the pipe, the water would not move through with such dynamic force.

The divine uses us as beacons of light. There are some substances that can detain and obstruct the flow of light through our physical bodies, thus interfering with our service as those beacons. These substances can have a negative effect on our electromagnetic field. We lower our vibratory rate to such an extent that we forfeit the power we have as masters to raise the vibrations of our environment or the people and circumstance within it.

It is no secret or surprise these same substances are known to trigger disease and illness. Some of the all-too-familiar culprits are animal products (including dairy), alcohol, excess sugar and drugs. The category of drugs is broad, including tobacco, coffee, prescription drugs as well as narcotics and street drugs.

Animal Products

If we are what we eat, then it is no wonder war has been such a constant in the history of mankind. When we ingest an animal, we take on some of that being's vibratory actions. Many of the animals we eat experience fear at the time of slaughter. Aggression and fear are major components in the making of war.

If we are what we eat, then what does eating these dead animals make of us?

There is extensive information available about the effects of foods on our vibrational frequencies. Among one of my favorite books on the subject is *Alkalize or Die* by Theodore A. Baroody. It is a straightforward and practical guide for those intending to honor the body's function as a pure temple. Live, whole foods contribute to our evolution as they raise the quality and quantity of our energy system. Dead, unwholesome foods work against our evolution. The idea is to give the body the purest, life-sustaining substances available in order to offer ourselves to the divine as pure vessels of light and masters of our physical existence.

In the *Essene Gospel of Peace, Book One,* Jesus speaks:

"So eat always from the table of God; the fruits of the trees, the grain and grasses of the field, and the honey of bees. For everything beyond these is of Satan, and leads by the way of sins and of disease unto death. But the foods which you eat from the abundant table of God give strength and youth to your body, and you will never see disease."

Chapter 12:
INNER FREEDOM

You live that you may learn to love. You love that you may learn to live. No other lesson is required of Man.

— *Jacquelyne Small*
Transformers

On the mental, emotional and psychological levels, the road to mastery demands we face and free ourselves from those issues that can make our journey more of a struggle than a joy. This requires inner work—inner work for not only the spirit, but the psyche as well.

All too often we try to avoid the inevitable pain of moving through the inner barriers that can keep us from our higher selves. The platitude still stands true: "We must go through it to grow through it."

In their book *The Wisdom of the Enneagram*, Riso and Hudson explain:

"Without self knowledge, we will not get very far on our spiritual journey, nor will we be able to sustain whatever progress we have made. One of the great dangers of transformational work is that the ego attempts to sidestep deep psychological work by leaping into the transcendent too soon."[22]

In my experience, some spiritual work does hold the power to literally dissolve, consume and thereby transcend dysfunctions of the personality. It requires great faith and determination to apply this work to the extent that it can ac-

135

tually facilitate such a miraculous healing. Those of us who are devoted to a spiritual practice may often find ourselves being led, perhaps through profound synchronicity, to the type of therapeutic work perfect for us.

Keeping our attention on the divine is paramount to spiritual growth. Therefore it is important to be aware of the activities within us that would readily grasp any opportunity to shove psychological issues deeper into the hidden recesses of the unconscious mind. In other words, if given voice, the psyche and the ego defenses would sound something like, "Now's our chance—while nobody's looking, let's bury this pain so deep they'll forget it's here, then we can really run the show and they'll never suspect."

However, the spirit and the psyche are so intimately entwined that when we are on a spiritual path, if we are brave enough to dive in and face our issues, the spirit will assist in big ways. If we take five steps, God and Goddess will carry us another ten steps or more.

The dysfunctional core issues and beliefs (we all have some) driving us and defining the windows through which we view the world and everyone in it must, at some point on our path, be addressed and become a partner in the very intimate process of self-development and inner work. These issues and beliefs that determine and thereby narrowly define our perception of who we are and how the world interacts with us can, if left unattended, keep us from acknowledging our oneness and embracing our mastery.

Even when one has had several years of such inner work and moved through the initial (and oftentimes most painful) layers of these core beliefs, there is always more to explore and transcend. The proverbial spiral staircase is perpetual. Each landing of the staircase holds another gift from our psyche, perhaps in some form of the same issues we've dealt with numerous times before. These gifts lie open within us to be handled and integrated as opportunities for exquisite metamorphosis.

We are a work in progress. We can never become too awake.

Chapter 13:
BEYOND COMPETING
AND COMPARING

*Each point of view matters; every request is granted; and
as the amazing universe unerringly expands, there is no end
to the Universal resources that fulfill these requests. And
there is no end to the answers to the never-ending stream of
questions—and for that reason, there is no competition.*
> — *Jerry and Ester Hicks*
> *Ask and It Is Given*

As we search through our baggage for ways to lighten our load a couple more things can be put aside: competing and comparing

Competing and comparing can be reduced to one common denominator—the singularly haunting question—"Am I good enough?" While on a spiritual journey, we can slip into the ego's trap of viewing others as either a threat to our spiritual status or a reassurance of it.

Our thoughts might be something like, "They must be closer to God than I am because they had that miracle happen to them," or "I am more powerful than he is, I have more business or more blessings or fewer problems," or "Am I as good or holy as she is? She has such clear intuition and I don't."

When we face ourselves, we begin to see how often and in what ways we compare and compete in our spiritual arena, whether secretly in thought, or openly in word or action. We lapse into forgetfulness of what we are—children of God, a status beyond the pettiness of sibling rivalry.

God is equally close to each of us. Yet some of us are speeding along on the road to mastery while others are struggling at a snail's pace. This progress depends on our awareness, attention and vibration. All three of these are at our command.

Making comparisons and competing is counterproductive to our spiritual expansion because every time we put our attention on how far along someone *else* is or how close someone *else* is to God we divert our attention from our own mastery and compromise our vibration. We steal our attention from the divine and undergo the emotional process of measuring our self worth by someone else's progress. Then we compromise our vibrations by reacting to that process either through a sense of superiority, which threatens our humility, or through jealousy, which is a form of hate.

We lose the point when we compare ourselves to others. Each of us is on our own journey, with our own baggage. Some of us have accumulated one thing, some of us another, and have been doing so for several lifetimes. We will all be in each other's "place" at one time or another. We must because we are one, like cells in the huge body of the universe.

To compete with each other for spiritual superiority or compare ourselves with one another for the purpose of "ranking" would be like a drop of sea water at the bottom of the ocean floor, comparing itself to a drop riding the crest of a high wave. Should that drop feel inadequate because it is at the bottom or superior because it has attained such depth? Should the drop on the crest feel closer to the heavens than the other drop or jealous because the drop at the bottom of the ocean is closer to God's heart? Considering every drop eventually merges with every other drop, wouldn't any of these reactions simply be a waste of energy, attention, and vibration? Sooner or later those drops will exchange position in the vastness of the ocean.

We are all children of God/Goddess. Therefore we are all divine beings, with equal potential as masters, manifesting in our own unique way at our own present point in space and time. None better, none worse.

In order to free ourselves of the habitual activity of comparing and competing, it is helpful to first internalize at very deep levels the knowledge—not the suspicion or the hope— but the absolute knowingness that "I Am divine and you are divine." Once we remember and truly know who we are, we eliminate the nagging question, "Am I good enough?" which drives the need to compare and compete.

Once this awareness and knowledge is firmly planted within us, then it is simply a matter of noticing those times when we are competing or comparing in thought, word or deed, and then pivoting those thoughts, words and behaviors. At those times remind yourself of your glorious status as a child of God and a traveler on the road to mastery. Allow yourself to feel good enough or more than good enough, and invite love and compassion to flow through you and to your imagined competition.

Traveling without the weight of comparing and competing creates a much lighter journey.

PART IV
THE DESTINATION

The happiness of a man in this life does not consist in the absence but in the mastery of his passions.
— Alfred, Lord Tennyson

Chapter 14:
THE MYTH OF THE CRUCIFIXION

You came among us to teach us all what we were capable of becoming, and we did not want to accept this. You showed us that the power and the glory were within every person's reach, and this sudden vision of our capacity was too much for us. We crucified you, not because we were ungrateful to the Son of God, but because we were fearful of accepting our own capacity. We crucified you, fearing that we might be transformed into gods. With time and tradition, you came to be just a distant divinity, and we returned to our destiny as human beings.

— Paul Coelho
The Pilgrimage

Christian religions and therefore millions of people throughout the world hold the belief that Jesus died on the cross for our sins and in so doing, saved us.

Let's examine the possibility that some mythology was woven into the story of Christ's death. What if the idea Jesus died for our sins is a myth? And if He, in fact, did save us, what did He save us from? More sin? Surely not—we are still knee deep in the stuff.

What if Jesus did not die *for* our sins, but *because* of our sins? What if He died because of one sin in particular—murder? What if He died simply because we killed Him? (I have heard people say, "What's this 'we' business! I wasn't there.

I didn't crucify Him." That's true. We were not there in these present bodies. The "we" I use here is in reference to the mass consciousness to which we each belong. In the absence of these temporary, individual bodies, "we" are an ocean of consciousness encompassing all time. So the "we" who killed Christ is the same "we" who comprise all of mankind's past and present behaviors.

The premise that Jesus was supposed to be crucified through some divine setup has very conveniently placed limits on our perception about His presence here and distracted our attention from the mastery He came to offer us onto the crucifixion itself.

We are suckers for sensationalism.

Christ was tortured and killed through one of the most cruel and heinous means of execution in use at that time, and it has captured our attention ever since. The cross as a symbol of the crucifixion is prevalent and is intended to remind us of His martyrdom. How many symbols for the ascension do we see hanging around people's necks?

Numerous movies have been made about Jesus' time here. They focus mostly on the crucifixion. How many movies have been made primarily about the ascension? We continue to invest our energy and pour our attention into the crucifixion and, as we do so, we remain safely stuck in the base, violent, fearful consciousness that caused us to perform that tragic act in the first place.

He came to bring us fully into our mastery as divine beings. He came to raise us up to be what He was, and it terrified us, it confused us and we refused to accept ourselves as God/Goddess. So we killed Him, and continue to do so every time we sink into the darkness of the crucifixion by feeding it with our emotions and attention. We continue to deny Him every time we commit acts of violence, war or hate of any kind.

Jesus came to accomplish much more than a painful death. Perhaps He came to bring us into a permanent golden age and teach us how to ascend without going through physical death. Maybe He came to put an end to the false belief that we are limited in any way or there is such a thing as death.

Perhaps He had a very different story in mind. What if Jesus had been allowed to live? He could have taught us for many more years, as many as necessary to bring us to mastery. Then He could have taught us how to raise and transform the physical body into pure light so we could ascend into the higher octaves as divine beings, free of human limitations and without so-called death.

Yes, He came to save us, but we didn't give Him the chance. Yet, He did give us the truths we need to save ourselves. His message was clear, but it was too short-lived to achieve its full intention at that time.

Nonetheless, the divine plan must be fulfilled and He did ascend. And in doing so, He gave us the blueprint for our own ascension. Now if we would wholeheartedly shift our attention *from* the crucifixion *to* the ascension, the truths and lessons of how to use that blueprint would become increasingly clearer to us. If the mass consciousness of mankind would shift in attention, the ascended Jesus Christ could give us greater assistance to raise us into the destiny of life and the ascension, thus completing the mission he began so long ago.

Perhaps it is time we find the strength to abandon the myth that has protected us from our guilt and fear for so long. Perhaps it is time to ask ourselves: "What if ...?" In so doing, we would be forced to face our destiny as masters. We would be forced to go beyond the fear nailing us all to the cross as we live through cycle after cycle of struggle and turmoil.

When we let go of the concept that God planned the crucifixion, we are free to see the possible origin of mistrust and fear many people experience regarding God. (See Chapter 10 on Trust.) After all, what kind of God would bring his only child to Earth only to have him tortured and killed?

The various pagan religions in practice during Christ's time often worshipped gods believed to be very cruel and punishing. Sacrifice was a regular aspect of those religions. Was the idea that God the Father would carry out the divine plan in such a vicious way somehow an offshoot of those beliefs?

From this perception it is no wonder so many religions have an image of God as a personified male figure prone to sadistically punishing us and making us suffer if we don't please him. This also raises the question: If he masterminded the crucifixion of his son for our sins, he must want us to suffer, too, right? Thus, fear of God and identification with martyrdom, which reeks of guilt, has taken seed within many of us.

There is nothing divine about pain and suffering. Although some good may come from suffering, in and of itself suffering is not a holy act. We are more inclined to turn to God when we are in such a state, but it does not mean human suffering is a part of God's will. The vibrational frequency of these feelings is not harmonious with the love and peace that is the divine. God and suffering do not make a vibrational match. Yet when suffering is suffused with love and devotion, it ceases to be suffering. It becomes the transcendent offering Jesus experienced on the cross. What He endured was a profound demonstration of His love for us, a love that could only come to us from His divinity.

In looking at the crucifixion as a human act, and not a divine plan, there is another question begging to be asked, and has been asked for centuries: If human will sought His death, then why did He not defend Himself, prevent the crucifixion, save Himself and save us from committing such an atrocity?

Perhaps once we determined our action and fate in this matter, Jesus, in His infinite love for us, chose to use the cross as an example. Not as a means to cause distress and guilt, but as an example of how we, too, can experience resurrection and ascension.

Free will also plays a role in seeking answers to this question. Acceptance of Jesus and His message is equal to acceptance of our mastery. Both must be done from our desire, autonomously and consciously. We must intentionally claim our role as divine beings. Anything less disclaims such a status. The divine doesn't (and didn't) overrule our will. We needed to view Him then—as we need to view our mastery today—through deep inner desire, acceptance, devotion, and love.

Once God is willfully invited into our hearts, everything can change in an instant. If we freely open and yield to the entrance of divine power, then it can instantly override any lower-frequency vibrations. However, unless we desire that power, ask for it, and accept it into our lives, it will not happen. God will not force himself on us or interfere with free will. The crucifixion was entirely free of any such interference.

Christ didn't use His divinity as a bargaining tool. He didn't sell out His father when faced with His death, perhaps not because He was fulfilling God's plan, but because divine will is not to be used to sway free will. Even when Jesus healed the sick, He first asked if they wanted to be free of the affliction. Their desire and free acceptance of the miracle was required for the healing to take place.

We continue to be faced with the same choice we had then—to accept our mastery or to crucify it. By choosing to stay ignorant to our divinity, we choose the latter. This divine mastery is already a part of us, so we suffer the pain of self-annihilation every time we choose to ignore it. We reenact the crucifixion of Christ through the denial of our own true Christ power.

Another aspect of this enormous historical event is the great debate about who actually did it—the Jews or the Romans?

The controversial film *The Passion of Christ* put a spotlight on the debate. As thousands flocked to watch the sensationalized barbarism and uncensored violence of the crucifixion, they also turned to the exercise of blaming someone else for this act. At least one question comes to mind in regard to this who-did-it obsession: If Christ's crucifixion was a means of fulfilling God's plan and saving humanity, then why don't we honor and appreciate whoever played the role of executioner, instead of persecuting them for it? If, in fact, the crucifixion was a holy act of martyrdom, then why aren't the Jews (who have, in the past, been blamed as "the ones") actually thanked for their role in unfolding the divine plan?

The Jews did not crucify Jesus, nor did the Romans.

Human fear crucified Jesus.

The crucifixion was not the Passion of Christ.

The ascension was the Passion of Christ, along with all He taught through his presence.

Perhaps it is time we honor His love for us by honoring His true Passion.

Maybe it is time to set aside our fears and doubts and look more closely at the greatest gift he gave us. If we embrace Jesus' legacy, claim our inheritance, and turn our attention away from His death, which was truly not a death at all, we can yet fulfill the original divine plan that brought Jesus to us. We can each become the power of Christ as we turn our attention to the ascension and call Him to assist in raising us into our mastery.

Chapter 15:
THE ASCENSION

"Ascension – the process of fully remembering one's unity with God and the one Spirit that unites all people in brother and sisterhood. Those who ascend may bypass the death process, and their entire body may be lifted into Heaven along with their soul ..."

— *Doreen Virtue*
Archangels and Ascended Masters

Once upon a time, the Earth was the center of the universe. Explorers planned journeys and navigated travel in accordance with this well-known fact. Scientists hypothesized and theorized within the constraints of this knowledge. Men, women, and children everywhere lived in the security of this supreme position.

This story was their reality. This reality was their story.

Then one day, along came a man who brought with him a different story. His name was Galileo. The trouble was that Galileo was one of the few people in the seventeenth century to know this new and different story. His story, which was his reality, went something like this: The Earth is not the center of the universe. The sun is the center, and the Earth revolves around the sun. We on Earth do not occupy the most high and superior position as center of the universe.

This story was not well received. Galileo was persecuted, locked up far away from everyone so his story would not threaten the present reality and force unwanted change in the world.

One of the most beautiful things about truth is that it is not contingent upon belief. Our stories define our reality. However they do not affect the ultimate truth. The sun was the center of Galileo's universe then, although we know now it is only a minor star at the edge of a rather ordinary galaxy among billions, and hardly the center of the universe. Earth was not and is not the most important planet in the heavens.

Once upon a time, even long before Galileo's time, everyone worked hard, made money, paid taxes, and died. Children were raised to know and understand they were born to do these things; women and men both devotedly played their parts in this story. People were born, suffered, grew old, and died. This was their story. This was their reality.

Then one day along came a man with a different story. His name was Jesus. The trouble was that Jesus was just about the only person in those days to know a new and different story. It went something like this: We are born as supreme beings and masters of great power, capable of great joy, peace, and love. We can do whatever the spirit desires; we can have whatever the spirit wants; we can be whoever the spirit longs to be. All of this is ours without limit. God is a part of each of us and does not want us to suffer. There is no need for sickness or aging. And there is no such thing as death. We do not have to die.

This story was not well received. Jesus was persecuted and executed. The people stuck to their story, despite the fact their reality created a much tougher fate than the one Jesus offered. However, this did not alter the ultimate truth Jesus delivered. We did not have to suffer and die then, and we do not have to suffer and die now.

In both stories, as in all stories, the players were captive to the perceived reality because the people around them made them captive.

In the novel *Ishmael* by Daniel Quinn, Ishmael said "Even if you privately thought the whole thing was madness, you had to play your part, you had to take your place in the story."[23]

And most of us today are still taking our place in the story.

Death is our reality because the race consciousness dictates it is so. Centuries ago, Jesus Christ transcended death through his ascension and told us we can do so as well. But here we are, still buying into the old story.

As children, we all heard grown-ups say, "There are two things you can count on in life—death and taxes." We learn, even before we come kicking and screaming from the womb, that life is hard and we must live in fear of our doomed ending—death.

Why do we continue to finance, with our very souls, the old story when the new and different one is so much better? Why not accept the power Jesus' story offers us? Why not embrace our own transformation into beings of light? Why do we prefer to let our life force drain away and then bury the carcass to rot in the dirt?

This is where the concept of critical mass (as seen in the story of The Hundredth Monkey) becomes so critical. Enough of us must know, comprehend, and believe in the ascension in order for it to replace the old story.

Even though Christians accept Jesus' story, they put on the brakes and stop short of believing we, too, can ascend. What makes the ascension so difficult to accept? Is it the idea of the physical body transforming into pure light? Or is it the idea of what we must do and be to facilitate this change that keeps the ascension out of our belief system?

According to my understanding (which is limited because I have not yet had the experience), the ascension is the result of a lifetime of loving thoughts and feelings, devotion to our own divinity, and wise governing of the physical body.

At the time of the ascension, the vibratory action of the body is moving at such a high, fast rate it experiences a metamorphosis. It rises from the Earth's gravitational hold as it becomes pure light and moves into the higher realms of existence. The only thing separating us from the higher octaves and the beings who dwell within them is our vibrational frequency. During the ascension, that frequency makes its final change to bring us into the next level of existence.

Sounds like another story, doesn't it? Well, it is a story. But remember: our stories are our reality. I don't know about you, but I like this story a whole lot better than the one we've been playing out for so long. There must be some reason why Jesus' words and actions and his ascension have made such an impression on the world for so many centuries. Perhaps we know, deep within our inner beings, that this is more than just a story. Perhaps we know that this is our destiny. Perhaps we know that Jesus left us a map to the most precious treasure of all.

Once upon a time, there was a call that sounded throughout the land. It was a Call to Mastery. Whoever was brave enough to answer that call became powerful beyond imagination and lived forever in peace and joy.

MY STORY

I have received many blessings along the path of my spiritual development. These include, in particular, four remarkable spiritual and therapeutic practices: Unity, Sahaja Yoga, Rapid Eye Technology, and the Saint Germain "I Am" Activity. Together they have served as a map that has kept me on the road to mastery and has redirected me when I wandered from that road. Much of what I share in this book is rooted in these teachings.

Unity

In my late teens, I discovered Unity. Before that, my metaphysical knowledge came from studying masters and mystics such as Kahlil Gibran and William Blake, as well as practices including the Silva Method and the Rosicrucians.

However, these were solitary pursuits, which I performed and experienced alone.

Unity changed that. As its name promises, it united me with others who where also on the conscious path. Being with people who were of like mind added a phenomenal breadth to my view of life and my experience of myself as a divine being.

Unity—a nondenominational organization—was my first encounter with a spiritual organization that did not personify and worship God as being separate and external from us. Recognizing the God and Goddess within and embracing the power of that truth is at the very core of Unity's teachings.

I was privileged for a few years to attend the Unity services at Avery Fisher Hall in New York City, and bask in the vibration of love and wisdom embodied by Eric Butterworth. He was one of the earliest and most influential ministers in the Unity movement. Throughout the years I have also attended services in Houston, Phoenix, and Salt Lake City. The powerful programs, weekly classes, and services Unity offers honor the road to mastery with companionship and a clear light with which to keep our sights upon the truth.

I am particularly grateful to Unity for giving me a strong foundation in understanding and executing effective prayer, as well as teaching me so much about the art of manifestation.

Sahaja Yoga

Nearly twenty-five years ago, I was recovering from great emotional trauma, climaxing in an unsuccessful suicide attempt.

During that time, I attended an event that introduced me to a woman named Shri Mataji Nirmala Devi. She was the guest speaker and her topic was Sahaja Yoga.[24] That night, I knew I had found my home. I knew I would never again revisit the hell from which I was being freed. And indeed, Sahaja Yoga was my home for the next several years.

Shri Mataji is a powerful, loving guru from India. She is an incarnation of the female aspect of God/Goddess. Sahaja Yoga is a form of meditation that raises a divine energy within us called the kundalini. The kundalini opens the chakras and brings a person into a state of thoughtless awareness.

Back then, I had the good fortune of spending much precious time in the presence of Shri Mataji, watching, listening, and learning. Many of us lived together in ashrams, sacred homes in which we lived collectively. These ashrams fostered innocence in relationships—we were brothers and sisters and sex was only a small aspect of marriage, expected to be limited because of its drain on the attention. These homes also provided us the opportunity to face and conquer our egos, as cohabitation with several unrelated people can definitely challenge the "little self." Perhaps most important, we lived together for the joys of devotion. We meditated collectively and participated in profound ceremonies spoken and sung in Sanskrit, which honored in deep ways the magnificence of the deities and ascended masters.

Shri Mataji taught about vibrations, their importance, and how to manage them. She taught us that we are saints, with the power to still our minds and thus join our hearts with the divine.

I went to India on two separate pilgrimages, along with hundreds of other devotees. Shri Mataji guided us through the sacred, historical sites of southern India. Each time there were hundreds of us from all over the world. I witnessed and experienced numerous miracles during these spiritual treks and expanded into a consciousness that otherwise would have been unreachable.

Those years with Sahaja Yoga blessed me with the visceral experience of our oneness with God and Goddess. They helped set a foundation for a relationship with the Divine that serves me still.

This work has been sprinkled with some of the techniques and insights from Sahaja Yoga that have helped to keep me on the road to mastery.

Rapid Eye Technology

In September, 1999, I found myself sitting across from a woman who was waving a plastic stick in front of my face. Her name was Carol Tuttle and the stick was an eye-directing device called a wand.

Carol was waving her wand in front of my eyes in what is known as the neurolinguistic programming (NLP) modalities. This movement of the wand, along with rapid blinking, movement of the eyes, and verbal statements, stimulates the brain to heal with amazing accuracy, speed, and efficiency.

Rapid Eye Technology (RET) is a nontraditional, therapeutic method of releasing emotional, mental, physical, and spiritual imbalances, patterns, issues, or problems on any level.[25] Anything from the effects of damaging trauma to simple stress can be quickly, easily, painlessly, and permanently lifted from one's cellular makeup and replaced with vibrational information that aligns with one's own higher self. Carol's book, *Remembering Wholeness: A Handbook for the 20th Century,* is based on her experiences as a rapid eye technician.[26]

Somewhere around my third or fourth session with Carol, I received a very powerful message from deep within myself. I had recently been practicing a daily routine of prayer and meditation revolving around a deep desire: "Dear God, how can I serve you above all things? Show me how I can best serve the Light now."

I unquestioningly expected an answer and so it came: I studied, practiced, and became certified as a rapid eye technician.

RET is gaining much popularity as an alternative therapy. The field of energy psychology in general provides healing for many people who, after years of traditional psychotherapy, are still struggling with mental health issues.

Of course, with the right therapist, psychotherapy can be an important tool for our well-being. Many years ago it played a vital role in my life. However, I have found the results of a few RET sessions can have as much or more healing effect as many years of traditional therapy.

I once heard Marianne Williamson (a popular author and spiritual leader) talk about the imperative need for us to get over our past *right now* and claim our greatness *right now* because we are running out of time. It felt as if this truth settled itself within me. In a deep way I understood that we could no longer afford to stay small, licking our wounds, year after year, in a world where spiritual giants are need-ed—*right now*.

Dr. Ranae Johnson, the founder of the Rapid Eye Institute in Portland, Oregon, is a most remarkable woman. In her book *A Winter's Flower,* she describes in detail how RET unfolded itself before her as a gift from the universe. At the time she was developing a treatment for her autistic son. That was about thirty years ago. In her second book, *Rapid Eye Technology,* Dr. Johnson shares the hows, whats and whys of this revolutionary form of energy work.

It is no wonder such a powerful tool for transformation appeared at a time when our consciousness was showing ap-parent signs of readying itself for the incoming golden age. (See Part I, Chapter 3.)

There are various forms of energy work and healing methods available to us today and more are coming in all the time. The floodgates have opened and we are being show-ered with many ways and means to move past our obstruc-tions and raise our consciousness to new heights.

A word of caution, though, as many of you may have learned by now: discrimination is the key. There are those who call themselves healers, but would take your money and leave your energy system in a mess if you give them the opportunity. I recommend Rapid Eye Technology, not only with unconditional confidence, but also a deep longing that you will pursue it and receive the benefits of working with a rapid eye technician.

Prior to coming to Suriname as a Peace Corps volunteer, I enjoyed a full-time practice as a rapid eye technician. My practice was thriving and exciting because each session held, for both the client and me, a space clearly being honored and assisted by the angels and cosmic beings. Words like "miraculous" and "unbelievable" were often used to describe the results of our sessions.

If you are answering the call to mastery, and truly desire to step into the full power of mastery, I sincerely recommend you find a rapid eye technician. There are several listed on the web site, www.rapideyetechnology.com. Use discretion here. Dr. Johnson teaches that we can be instrumental in the healing of others only to the degree to which we are healed ourselves. So, work with someone with whom you resonate and respect.

Your mastery will come much faster and easier once you are free from limiting information etched into your cells, either through genetics, past lives or present trauma. The fewer discordant memories we have tugging at our attention and directing our behavior, the freer we are to turn a more pure and powerful attention toward achieving mastery.

Some of the techniques and insights I have shared with you are from Dr. Johnson's teachings and from my experiences as a rapid eye technician.

RET has cleared the way for me to more fully focus my love and joy on attaining mastery and the ascension.

The Saint Germain "I Am" Activity

About three years ago, a dear friend and gifted intuitive placed a book in my hands and said, "Tell me how that feels." We were often checking the vibrations of things like books or vitamins or photographs, so this was not an unusual request.

I can remember gasping as I felt the radiation pouring from that book.

I knew this was something I wanted to read. It was the first book in a series, called *Unveiled Mysteries*, by Godfre Ray King. As my friend explained, it is rather difficult to find in most bookstores—someone had recently given the book to him and mentioned the best source was the Saint Germain Foundation.[27]

I immediately made a note of the address and phone number and called to place my order the next day.

The first thing to be said about Saint Germain's "I Am" Activity is there's not much I can say. I do not have the authority to translate or interpret any of the information contained within the many works of the Saint Germain Foundation (based in Chicago, Illinois), nor does anyone else.

These books, tapes, CDs and periodicals contain the dictations given to us directly by Saint Germain and several other ascended masters. These dictations are detailed instructions on how to attain full mastery and gain the ascension in this lifetime. These were dictated through Mr. and Mrs. Godfrey Ballard in the 1930s, '40s and '50s.

There are many Sanctuaries throughout America and the world, each with a leader who facilitates ceremonies and services using only the exact words of the masters. There is no personal counseling or teaching involved independent of the instruction given by the masters.

Saint Germain was very clear about maintaining the purity of His work by requesting it never be filtered through any human interpretation of any kind. Saint Germain's teachings are based on the recognition, acknowledgement and devotion to one's own "I Am" presence.

When Moses asked God for a name to pass on to his people, God answered, "Tell them I Am that I Am." The "I Am" presence is the individualized power of God in action, within each of us; it is a highly evolved state of consciousness.

Using the holy phrase "I Am" followed by sincere, empowering words will reconstruct the cellular base of your self-image and identity. Almost all of the RET reframes (phrases replacing negative, core beliefs) begin with the words "I Am." Many institutions and teachings apply the divine name, "I Am." It is the claim to our personal divinity.

I have noticed that many of the teachings and writings known to us since these dictations were first published have been based on like principles. The language and delivery are different, but the principles are pretty much the same. It seems this powerful and ubiquitous work has quietly helped set the foundation for the study of truth in the modern world.

There is a good chance you may not be familiar with the "I Am" Activity. The Foundation does not solicit, advertise or attempt to convert. If one is ready and longing for one's mastery, they will find Saint Germain's work on their own—the radiation will attract them by some means. And when they find it, if they are ready for mastery, they will know they have found their freedom.

I find each day to be blessed by the potency of the words of these Loving masters. As I work to live by these principles, "I Am" becoming the light more fully and "I Am" moving forward on the road to mastery more joyfully.

Both Sahaja Yoga and the "I Am" Activity recognize the truth that we cannot pay for God. Therefore, aside from books and materials, there is no charge for learning or practicing these divine teachings from either of these organizations.

A GIFT

In the spirit of gratitude, I would like to offer a small gift for joining me on the road to mastery, if only for the brief time it has taken to read this book.

The following is a blessing entitled "A Prayer for Our Home." I am releasing this prayer from all copyright regulations and if it resonates with you, I am inviting you to use it freely. Get creative—enlarge it, frame it, beautify it in any way you choose and give it as a gift or place it in your own home.

I hope it fills your heart, and whatever space it occupies, with great Light and Love.

Thank you,

Paula Bronte

A PRAYER FOR OUR HOME

Dear God,
May this house be our Home.
May our home be a Sacred Place
Where Your Presence is known in every thought,
word and deed.
Protect us from darkness and doubt.
Allow only Light and Faith to pass our threshold.
Make this a Safe Place, a place of Healing.
Unite us with Abundance and let
Your Will and Your Love flow through us.
May the Angels of Peace, Harmony, and Prosperity
Dwell here among us always.
And may the Power of the Violet Flame blaze Eternally
So that all who enter this Sacred Place may know You and
be Joyful.
Amen

A Call to Mastery

ENDNOTES

Glossary

1 Carroll, Lee. *Kryon, A New Dispensation.* Del Mar, California: The Kryon Writings, Inc., 2004. The series of Kryon books are among the most profound and vibrationally powerful channeled works to come from the "new energy" that I have experienced. Another channeled work which I feel falls into this category of exception material is the Bartholomew series. Very inspiring information that contains many of the principles found in *A Course in Miracles* simply written and easy to understand. Among the channeled books of Bartholomew are: *Reflections of an Elder Brother, From the Heart of a Gentle Brother, and I Come As A Brother.*

2 Williamson, Marianne, *Everyday Grace.* New York: Penguin Putnam, 2002. I highly recommend *anything* by this author including CDs, especially if you would like to have a working knowledge of *A Course in Miracles.*

3 Mitchell, Stephen. *The Gospel According to Jesus.* New York: HarperCollins, 1991. A good read for anyone interested in learning more about Christ and his teachings. Mitchell offers us a "beyond the bible" version of the Master's time here on Earth.

4 Abraham-Hicks. *A New Beginning II.* San Antonio: Abraham-Hicks Publications, 1991. Abraham is a group consciousness speaking to us through Esther Hicks from another dimension. The channeled works from Abraham are the prime source for gaining a deep, practical understanding of the Law of Attraction. *A New Beginning I* and *II* were the first two books by Abraham. There have been several

others channeled since then. They are all valuable guides to learning the skill of manifesting. Their audios are also highly valuable tools for shifting into a consciousness of abundance. You can find them as well as a great monthly newsletter on their website, www.abraham-hicks.com.

Chapter 2: Global Purification and the Next Golden Age

5 *"I Am" Fundamental Series I.* Chicago: Saint Germain Foundation, Saint Germain Press, Inc. The first three books published by the Foundation are the place to start. These are channeled works of Saint Germain and other ascended masters that hold the power to greatly impact consciousness. I suggest that anyone who is truly interested in being a spiritual master read these books, the discourse series and use the decrees. This work was given to us nearly seventy years ago, so approach this material with an open mind—be willing and able to sift out whatever elements or language you perceive to be of the "old energy." Focus on the vibration you feel and the energy that moves through you as you work with this material, rather than any aspect that may feel too "old fashioned." I believe you will be astonished by the results.

6 This is the simplest, most straightforward explanation to which my pen can give expression. If you would like a more sophisticated and intricate look at the past cycles, you may want to find other sources of information. I have learned the less we indulge in intellectual overstatement, the more our hearts and minds can merge in the comprehension of spiritual concepts.

Chapter 3: The Three Levels of Mastery

7 Coelho, Paul. *The Pilgrimage.* New York: HarperCollins,

1995. The novels written by Mr. Coelho are insightful, profound journeys into spirituality and mysticism. In addition to *The Pilgrimage* I also recommend *The Alchemist*.

Chapter 4: Sex & Silly Putty

8 Through the use of RET, painful issues regarding sex can be cleared effectively. RET does not advocate abstinence. In my practice, I honor each person's choices and serve in a loving acceptance and support of those choices.

9 Hawkins, Dr. David R. *Power vs. Force.* Carlsbad, California: Hay House, 2002. This is a powerful, intellectual guide to understanding and using kinesiology. Reading Dr. Hawkins' work will increase your vibrational frequency while also teaching the importance of individual vibration and frequencies.

10 Walsch, Neale Donald. *Conversations with God.* New York: G.P. Putnam's Sons, 1996. I highly recommend any and all of the books in this series, no matter what stage of your metaphysical studies you are in. While reading these books, you will feel an intimate connection to the divine and clarity about who you really are.

11 Carr-Gomm, Philip and Stephanie. *The Druid Craft Tarot.* New York: St. Martin's Press, 2004.

12 Williamson, Marianne. *Everyday Grace.* New York: Penguin Putnam, 2002.

Chapter 5: The Chakra System

13 Thought Field Therapy web site, www.tftrx.com.

14 Emotional Freedom Technique web site, www.emofree.com.

Chapter 7: Formula #1 – Mastery

15 *Voice of the I Am*, August, 1994. Chicago: Saint Germain Press, Inc.

16 Hillenbrand, Laura. *Seabiscuit*. New York: Random House Ballantine, 2001.

17 *Time Magazine.* September 15, 2003.

Chapter 9: Formula #3 – The Conscious Path

18 Eden, Donna. *Energy Medicine*. New York: Penguin Putnam, Inc., 1999. Ms. Eden is a master healer. I use information from this book in my practice as well as my daily life. Visit her website for information about her workshops and her Energy Medicine Kit.

Chapter 10: Formula #4 – The Simple Stuff

19 Eden, Donna. *Energy Medicine*. New York: Penguin Putnam, Inc., 1999.

20 Abraham-Hicks. *A New Beginning II.* San Antonio: Abraham-Hicks Publications, 1991.

21 Christina Baldwin. *Life's Companion; Journal Writing as a Spiritual Quest.* New York: Bantam, 1990.

Chapter 12: Inner Freedom

22   Riso, Don Richard and Hudson, Russ. *The Wisdom of the Enneagram.* New York: Bantam Books, 1991. The enneagram is a psychological categorizing and study of personality types and how they relate to our spirituality. It can be "heady" work, but a fascinating way to learn more about yourself and how to relate to others.

Chapter 15: The Ascension

23   Quinn, Daniel. *Ishmael.* New York: Bantam/Turner, 1992. A very insightful novel about our behavior here on Earth as a species. Although it was written fifteen years ago this is a perfect time in our evolution to check this one out. It offers a keen view of our attitude toward the planet and other species and is motivational in changing how we inhabit or beloved Earth.

My Story

24 Sahaja Yoga web site, www.sahajayoga.com.

25 Rapid Eye Technology web site, www.rapideyetechnology.com.

26 Carol Tuttle, www.caroltuttle.com.

27 Saint Germain Foundation web site, www.saintgermainfoundation.org.

ABOUT THE AUTHOR

Paula Bronte is a Master Rapid Eye Technician in private practice in the Seattle area. She has worked in the field of energy healing since 1998. Paula also holds a certification in Thought Field Therapy. TFT is the original form of energy tapping—a technique which releases emotion by tapping acupressure points in specific sequences.

Reading *The Prophet* by Kahlil Gibran when she was fifteen years old launched Paula on a lifetime of spiritual and philosophical study and practice. She holds a B.A. in philosophy from Brooklyn College. As a devotee of Shri Mataji Nirmala Devi, Paula traveled to India twice and lived in ashrams for many years, practicing a sacred form of meditation called Sahaja Yoga.

Paula worked in sales and management for twelve years. After leaving the corporate world, she developed a full-time RET practice where she focused on helping clients heal and reclaim their divine wholeness. During this time she studied the teachings of Saint Germain and became closely acquainted with the Ascended Masters and their healing powers. Paula then spent two years serving in the Peace Corps in Suriname, South America, while writing this book.

Contact Paula Bronte at:
www.acalltomastery.com
acalltomastery@yahoo.com

Printed in the United States
202136BV00001B/55-102/P